Library of
Davidson College

Foreign and Comparative Studies/African Series XXIX

On His Majesty's Service in Uganda:
The Origins of Uganda's African Civil Service, 1912 - 1940

by Nizar A. Motani

Maxwell
School of Citizenship
and Public Affairs
Syracuse University

For two decades the Maxwell School has had as a major thrust of its teaching and research programs a concentration upon the world outside our national borders. In 1975 this commitment to foreign and comparative studies stands as a *sine qua non* of our intellectual endeavors. Increasingly the scholar and teacher is obliged to consider the influences on his work from outside our borders in order to diminish the culture-bound nature of the social sciences.

Maxwell's organization for teaching and research purposes emphasized discrete areas of the world: Soviet and East Europe, Latin America, Eastern Africa and South Asia. In addition, numerous faculty members have come here with interests in Western European countries and subjects. During the fifties and sixties, grants to subsidize a variety of such programs and interests came abundantly to Maxwell as to many other universities. That day is now gone — in fact, the scarcity of funds for supporting teaching and research about the rest of the world is a disturbing reality. As the pressures for neo-isolationism grow, as the energy shortage and related "crises" unfold, the university should feel even more sharply its extra-national role.

The Foreign and Comparative Studies Program is the present expression of Maxwell's awareness of the imperative for attention to foreign and international questions. This Program coordinates and supervises undergraduate and graduate concentrations which involve comparative and area studies. It encourages and motivates faculty cooperation in inter-regional research and teaching more effectively to meet the demands and opportunities of the present day.

The Foreign and Comparative Studies Monograph Series is a central part of this enterprise. It subsumes the series previously published by the Eastern African Studies Program and envisions an expansion of the output from the Latin American, South Asian, Soviet and East European and Western European faculties. Today, Maxwell has a large number of faculty members whose research interests include these areas. This series is a medium for their publishing manuscripts scheduled to appear in standard journals at a later date, monographs too long to appear in journals and yet not of book length, and other items. Scholars elsewhere are invited to submit their manuscripts for consideration for publication as parts of the series.

Chairmen, Publications Committee — African Studies
                                                      Roderick Macdonald
                                                      James L. Newman

Editorial Advisory Committee — Foreign and Comparative Area Studies

    Guthrie Birkhead, Chairman   Robert Kearney
    Edwin Bock   Ronald McDonald
    Robert Gregory   Marshall H. Segall
    Robert Jensen

Publishing Desk
211 Maxwell School
Syracuse University
Syracuse, New York 13210
USA

ON HIS MAJESTY'S SERVICE IN UGANDA:
THE ORIGINS OF UGANDA'S AFRICAN CIVIL
SERVICE, 1912-1940

by
Nizar A. Motani

FOREIGN AND COMPARATIVE STUDIES/AFRICA XXIX
MAXWELL SCHOOL OF CITIZENSHIP AND PUBLIC AFFAIRS
SYRACUSE UNIVERSITY

1977

Copyright

1978

by

MAXWELL SCHOOL OF CITIZENSHIP AND PUBLIC AFFAIRS

SYRACUSE UNIVERSITY, SYRACUSE, NEW YORK, U.S.A.

Library of Congress Cataloging in Publication Data
  Motani, Nizar.   On His Majesty's Service in Uganda.
  Foreign and Comparative Studies: Africa: 34
  Bibliography:p.
  1. Civil service--Uganda--History.
  2. Africanization--Uganda--History.
  I. Title., II. Series: Foreign and Comparative Studies: African Series: 34.
  JQ2951.A66M67   354'.676'1006   78-4877
  ISBN 0-915984-51-2

To My Parents

and

Yasmin

ABOUT THE AUTHOR

Nizar A. Motani is an Assistant Professor of History at Bowdoin College, Brunswick, Maine. He received his Ph.D. in History from the School of Oriental and African Studies at the University of London. Born in Uganda, he has lectured extensively on the plight of East Africa's Asian refugees. An article on this subject appeared in 1975 in the Kenya Historical Review.

Introduction

This essay offers the first detailed history of the African Civil Service (ACS) in Uganda from 1912 to 1940. In doing so, it gives new insight into African initiatives in the Uganda Protectorate Administration. It further suggests that certain established views on the interwar period in Uganda need to be corrected.

Africans in the racially-structured Uganda Civil Service (UCS)--composed of European, Asian and African branches--held mostly subordinate or menial positions until the 1940s. This probably led to the assumption that the African staff could not have commanded much influence in the UCS. Partly for this reason, it seems, scholarly attention has been given to collaborators and opponents of colonial administration who mainly operated outside the central government. Thus the activities of the chiefs (Fallers, 1964; Low & Pratt, 1960; Twaddle, 1969), the Baganda agents (Twaddle, 1967; Roberts, 1962); the traditional authorities (Richards, 1960), the mass "populist" movements (Apter, 1967; Low, 1971; Lonsdale, 1968) and the post-war nationalists and politicians (Low, 1971) have all been accorded varying degree of importance.

During the late 1950s and the early 1960s, as a growing number of African countries approached independence, their civil services aroused considerable scholarly interest. Britain's dependencies were administered through the local colonial bureaucracies which collectively made up the Colonial Service--and the Colonial Service was the main instrument of British imperial authority (Jefferies, 1938). The transfer of power meant preparing indigenous officers to fill as many senior posts as possible in their respective civil services. This process, which has been termed "Africanization" or "localization," has been the subject of two books: A. L. Adu's <u>The Civil Service in New African States</u> (Adu, 1965), and Richard Symond's <u>The British and their Successors</u> (1966)--the British efforts to train East Africans to take over from the expatriates are discussed at some length in these books; these discussions cover many countries and essentially only survey, rather than provide a detailed picture of, the process of Africanization.

In the specific case of Uganda there are three theses that portray the problems connected with propelling Uganda towards independence with an Africanized civil service: C. J. Bryant's Some Problems of Public Administration in Uganda (London, Ph.D. thesis, 1963); A. F. M. Evans' The Africanisation of the Civil Service in Uganda (Manchester, M.A. thesis, 1964) and D. A. Gugin's Africanization of the Uganda Public Service (Wisconsin, Ph.D. thesis, 1967). Taken together these dissertations adequately document and analyze the problems, policies and legacies of the British Administration regarding Africanization from 1940 to 1964; however, the period before 1940 has been touched upon only sketchily. This study provides a detailed history of Uganda's African Civil Service up to 1940 and at the same time serves as a background to the Africanization programs implemented during the decade preceding independence in 1962.

In addition to documenting a missing section in the colonial administrative history of Uganda, this study of the ACS questions certain assumptions about the interwar period. The Protectorate Administration of Uganda has been generally accepted as a "British affair" (Pratt, 1965) and African political activity has been identified with the chiefs and the native authorities. The present conventional wisdom appears to be that the African staff was neither influential nor very active or concerned with changing the racial structure of the UCS devised by the British. But a further examination of the UCS makes it evident that there was much tension in it and actual conflicts involving all three racial groups occurred fairly frequently.

Activities of Uganda's African civil servants clearly indicate that African initiative was not absent during the period 1919-1940. What John Iliffe wrote about Tanganyikan Africans in the early years of German rule also applies to Africans in the Uganda Protectorate Administration:

"...Africans were not the passive objects of colonial rule, unable to influence their fate or to respond rationally to new situations."[1]

---

[1] John Iliffe, Tanganyika Under German Rule, 1905-1912, Cambridge, 1969, p. 5.

Another commonplace of scholars as well as politicians has been that the unpopularity of the Asians resulted from their control over retail and wholesale trade and the Africans' inability to compete with them in the commercial arena (Morris, 1968; Low, 1971; Apter, 1967; Ghai and Ghai, 1970). Though this cannot be denied, the origin of at least part of this anti-Asian bias of the African leaders can probably be traced to the antagonism between African and Asian staff in the UCS during the 1920s. The political movements of the 1940s and the nationalist parties of the 1950s in Uganda were markedly hostile toward the Asians. But it should be emphasized that many of the future chiefs and politicians commenced their public careers as civil servants in the Protectorate Administration.

The Asian factor in the Administration also has been underrated. The established view suggests that the Asians, if not engaged in trade or skilled private employment, worked as subordinate civil servants (Morris, 1968; Ghai & Ghai, 1970); however their subordinate status did not prevent them from exercising direct and indirect influence over the policy of Africanization. Brought to Uganda for reasons of expediency, they were entrenched in the Administration by the outbreak of the First World War. Africanization meant the gradual elimination of the Asian clerical service. The Asian clerks countered this threat by demonstrating the excellence of their work to their European superiors and by manipulating the clerical training schemes for Africans which British officers unwisely delegated to them. Largely as a result of this, many European officers in Uganda were reported to have shown a "temperamental inability to work with African staff."[1] Indeed, there are indications that a tacit alliance to this end developed between European and Asian staff during the interwar years, ostensibly to maintain "the efficiency and standards" of the Uganda Civil Service.

In this struggle for lucrative positions and the retention of privileged status, racial prejudice and insults came into play.

---

[1] Colonial Office (C.O.) 685/25, Executive Council (Exco) minutes, 9.24.38.

The immigrant communities resorted to emphasizing their moral and cultural distinctiveness in order to justify the exclusion of Africans from more responsible appointments in the UCS. This device proved eminently useful and was evoked frequently in order to stifle measures likely to upset the status quo in favor of the Africans. Such racialism and paternalism inevitably militated against African advancement. Nevertheless, the paternalism and the racial arrogance of the foreigners met with an early African response. Informed African opinion demanded higher education up to university level in 1921, and African civil servants started a campaign for equality with non-Africans in 1922. It was their skillful negotiations and sustained pressure that helped to bring about, in 1940, the beginnings of a non-racial meritocracy and higher academic education in Uganda. Until then, the educational system was deliberately retarded by the British. (Motani, 1976)

Finally, the changing fortunes of the African civil service illuminate the great extent of control exercised by the Imperial Government in London over the minutiae of purely local schemes well after Uganda became financially self-sufficient in 1915. The Protectorate Government could not spend its revenues in the manner it wished without the approval of Whitehall. The British Treasury virtually directed the priorities of the Uganda Administration until 1928, while London officials at the Colonial Office were similarly inclined toward imposing their views on the man-on-the-spot.

The Early African Personnel

With the creation of the Uganda Protectorate in 1894-96, the British had to recruit a variety of civil servants to administer their latest dependency. Until the 1940s, the Protectorate Government Establishment was essentially a non-African domain, except at the lower rungs. The two categories of Africans, namely the saza (county) chiefs, especially in Buganda, and the Baganda agents outside Buganda, were not designated as Protectorate officials. Though under the direct supervision of District Officers and responsible for enforcing Protectorate Government legislation, the saza chiefs were identified with the native administrations. (Low & Pratt, 1960)

Government by Baganda agents represented a transitional phase in the British attempt to administer Uganda with a minimum of European officers. The Baganda agents were temporary expedients, and their withdrawal from different parts of Uganda left the Protectorate Government's administrative establishment in the hands of the British. (Twaddle, 1967; Roberts, 1962)

In India, at this time, Indian civil servants were starting to agitate against their exclusion from the Indian Civil Service, which had been filled with British recruits only, since the 1860s. In Uganda, Africans of administrative class were members of the native governments which were African in character from the outset. Tribal authorities and the missions could absorb most of the ambitious and talented Africans. There was no question of African administrators entering the corresponding grades in the Protectorate Government. Thus, while in India local men were struggling in the second decade of the twentieth century to penetrate the administrative ranks of their civil service and achieve equality of opportunity with the British, in Uganda the handful of skilled Africans in the Central Government did not even have specific or regular terms of employment. Had the African chiefs been treated as senior members of the Protectorate Administration, then the total number of Africans in the upper grades would have been significant and they together would have formed an important interest group. Such a group probably would have required a set of regulations governing their conditions of employment. However, since the chiefs, who were in reality senior African civil servants with great responsibility, were not regarded as a part of the Protectorate Service, the creation of an African civil service would primarily involve clerks and interpreters because they were the next important African element in the Protectorate Government. Hence, the African civil service would, in the first place, aim at transforming clerks and interpreters from casual employees into permanent civil servants.

From the late 1910s, African artisans, technicians, agricultural assistants and others who manned the field services were employed under departmental regulations. The middle and junior level posts, clerical as well as technical, that could not be filled locally by Africans, were held by Asian personnel recruited from India. In reality a version of the three-tier administrative structure that had earlier been suggested by Lord Lugard and Sir Harry Johnston had emerged in Uganda by 1912. It was seen to be an economical way of administering the country; each of the three racial groups in the British Empire contributing according to its ability. The absence of educated or skilled Africans in Uganda had caused the middle tier to be filled by Asians from India. On climatic, racial and financial grounds, the top tier was very small and reserved for the Europeans. (Cairns, 1965; Motani, 1972)

Early British Thoughts on the Native Civil Service (NCS)

The first official scheme for the Africanization of the civil service, put forward for discussion in January 1912, was concerned with the subordinate clerical establishment. Its architect was the Second Assistant Secretary, G. Lyall, who was perturbed by the "annually increasing" cost of employing Indian clerks. He felt the necessity for:

> "...the formulation of some scheme for the training of native clerks with the ultimate object of the Civil Service of Uganda being composed only of Europeans and natives."

Lyall then outlined the ways and means of training African clerks and suggested how government employment could be made more attractive for them.[1] While the most economical and effective method of training African clerks was being considered, the question of retaining the few African clerks and interpreters in government service had become extremely important.

---

[1] Uganda National Archives, Secretariat Minute Paper (U.N.A.S.M.P.) 2351, minute 1, G. Lyall to Chief Secretary (C.S.), 1.15.12.

Accordingly, in December 1913 Governor Frederick Jackson appointed a Native Civil Service Committee (NCSC) chaired by Chief Justice W. Morris Carter. Its task was "to consider the question of the permanent employment of Native Clerks and Interpreters in the Service of the Protectorate." The NCSC's recommendations included provision of free quarters for single men; free quarters plus a plot of land to grow food for married men; free transport when traveling on duty and to or from leave; a local traveling allowance, one month's leave each year and pension on retirement at the age of 45.[1]

The liberality of the NCSC's proposals drew an admonitory letter from the Colonial Office ruling out any hopes of Treasury sanction unless the recommendations were considerably watered down. The outbreak of the First World War, moreover, became a new setback for the entire scheme which was to be shelved "until normal conditions are restored."[2]

While the Protectorate Government was waiting for the right time to revise the NCSC's proposals, 18 African clerks and interpreters in government offices at Kampala took the unprecedented step of petitioning the Governor for stabilized terms of employment in March 1918. The signatories to this petition included two names which should be noted since they recur in connection with subsequent African political activity. They were Joswa Kamulegeya, the Budo*-educated son of an important saza chief, and Sepiriya Kadumukasa, another of Katikiro (Chief Minister

---

[1] Colonial Office (C.O.) 536/69, No. 304, Ag. Governor to Secretary of State for the Colonies (S. of S.), 6.29.14. The NCSC believed that "the efficient working life" of Ugandan Africans was unlikely "to extend beyond 45 years of age." The basis of this belief, however, was not stated.

[2] U.N.A.S.M.P. 3597, min. 38, memorandum signed by Carter, 9.9.15.

*Budo, in Buganda, was the site of a Protestant (CMS) school later known as King's College Budo. This prestigious institution offered primary and junior secondary education until full secondary education was added in the 1930s.

of Bugunda) Apolo Kagwa's British-educated sons. The petitioners showed a good understanding of the privileges enjoyed by those Asian clerks and the less than half a dozen African clerks serving under the 1912 Regulations.[1] Referring to themselves, the petitioners observed:

> Hitherto, there has been no attempt on the part of the Government to ameliorate and put on a proper basis the conditions of service of the Native Clerks and Interpreters; whilst some of these are being quite well paid, others are very meagrely paid with no hope of promotion. In certain cases the rate of pay is far below the amount of work they are called upon to perform.

African terms of service were generally in the hands of the departmental heads who normally rebuffed all African requests for leave, promotion or salary increments. These and numerous other grievances had compelled them to supplicate the Governor to "cause a Native Clerical Staff to be formed with equal privileges as those...for the Asiatics." The petitioners argued that although they were "natives of the Protectorate", they were "equally British subjects" and therefore entitled to the same rights and privileges enjoyed by other British subjects.[2] Their emphasis was on equality in status rather than on similar salaries.

Serwano Kulubya and Blasio Kagwa, the two most respected, able and senior African civil servants, had already been placed under the 1912 Regulations for non-European subordinate personnel. Hence, they were not associated with this petition which marked the first attempt by some African employees of the Protectorate Government at organized, collective bargaining. The pattern for future African political activity within the Civil Service of

---

[1] Ibid., min. 52, Native Clerks and Interpreters to Governor, 3.20.18. The 1912 Regulations, also known as Terms of Service for Members of the Non-European Clerical Staff of the Uganda and East Africa Protectorates, September 1912, Govt. Printer, Entebbe, were designed for Asians recruited overseas. However, the salary scale of the 1912 Regulations was made applicable to certain meritorious Africans.

[2] U.N.A.S.M.P. 3597, min. 52, para. 3-4.

Uganda was created in 1918. It was to center on the registration of protest and exercise of pressure on the Government through petitioning and negotiating to change its policy. Kamulegeya and his fellow petitioners were informed that the Government would take up the Native Civil Service (NCS) scheme after the war had ended.

When World War I ended, Kamulegeya reopened correspondence regarding the position of native clerks and interpreters. This time he wrote privately to P. W. Cooper, the Provincial Commissioner for Buganda, in whose office he was an interpreter. Cooper was requested to present the matter to the Government before he went on leave, and his sympathetic attitude set the ball rolling. The Chief Secretary was asked to appoint another committee to consider definite conditions of service for all skilled and educated natives in government employment.[1] Carter's NCSC of 1913 was soon resurrected and its report was requested before the arrival of Sir Alfred Lascelles.

Lascelles had been sent by the Colonial Office to investigate the question of the salaries of European and Asian civil servants in East Africa. A salary revision had become necessary as a result of the war. (Jeffries, 1938) The announcement of the Lascelles visit to East Africa seemed to have a dramatic effect on non-African civil servants. Since their conditions of service were the subject of his mission, European and Asian civil servants organized themselves into formal bargaining bodies.[2] Hitherto the European personnel was normally called the "European Staff" or "European Officers", while the Asian employees of the Government were called the "Non-European Subordinate Staff", the "Asiatic Subordinate Staff" or the "Asiatic Clerical Service." After March 1919, with the formation of the European Civil Service Association and the Asiatic Civil Service Association, the terms "European Civil Service" and "Asiatic Civil Service" seem to have

---

[1] Ibid., min. 66, Cooper to C.S., 1.24.19.

[2] U.N.A.S.M.P. 5640, min. 1, Asiatic C.S. Ass. (ACSA), Entebbe, to C.S., 4.1.19; ibid., min. 5, A.C.S.A. to Governor, 6.17.19; the Uganda Herald, 3.21.19, p. 10.

become fairly standard. Representatives of both these associations communicated their respective grievances to Lascelles. African employees in the Government had no regular or definite terms of service and Lascelles had not been instructed to consider their position. Perhaps, lacking this external stimulus, the Africans then failed to form an association similar to those formed by the Europeans and Asians. However, Lascelles did declare the need to build up an African civil service in Uganda in order to run the country more economically.[1] He further commented on the poverty of East Africa's educational facilities. Without immediate improvement, he warned, the desirable replacement of Asian clerks by Africans would not be feasible.

Views expressed by Cooper and Lascelles were strongly echoed by the NCSC of 1919, which presented its report in January, 1920. It was recommended that candidates should serve for three years on agreement and should be made permanent and pensionable on confirmation. The salary structure divided the NCS into four grades embracing all clerks, artisans, technicians and professionals.[2] Where necessary, free quarters and plots of land (to grow food) were also recommended. However, local and traveling allowances were restricted to special cases as seen fit by the Governor. Free transport when on duty or when proceeding to and from leave, one month's leave each year, and pensions on all salaries of Rs. 40/- and upwards were the other salient features of the report. To qualify for pensions, at least 15 years service would be necessary, otherwise gratuities would be paid. Candidates could enter any grade according to ability and training; promotion to higher grades would be through examinations.

---

[1] C.O. 536/98, Lascelles to S. of S., 4.5.19.

[2] C.O. 536/99, Report, Part I, enc. in, Ag. Gov. (Carter) to S. of S., 1.15.20. Grade I - Rs. 65/- and upwards to Rs. 200/- per month, with annual increments of Rs. 5/- p.m.; Grade II - Rs. 40/- to Rs. 60/- p.m. with annual increments of Rs. 4/- p.m.; Grade III - Rs. 18/- to Rs. 38/- with annual increments of Rs. 2/- p.m. Rest of the employees would draw salaries in the range Rs. 5/- to Rs. 15/- p.m. 15 Rupees equalled £1.

African Initiative and Challenge to the Colonial Set-Up

Generally, Protectorate officials on the spot found that the views of remote Whitehall bureaucrats frustrated their NCS scheme and the two parties were to be drawn into prolonged negotiations before a compromise was reached in 1925. In the meantime, the African staff did what it could to ameliorate its plight.

African politics of protest and petitioning in Uganda were directly or indirectly tied up with the war. The increased cost of living resulting from the 1914-1918 war had provided the Africans in government employment with a further incentive to press their claims for increased salaries in 1919. Lascelles had strongly recommended a war-bonus of Rs. 4/- per month for certain types of Africans in government service--retroactive to April 1, 1918. European and Asian civil servants had enjoyed this supplementary benefit from April 1918, to meet the increased cost of living.[1] The Protectorate Government, however, had barred Africans from this relief-scheme, ostensibly on the grounds that they did not depend on imported goods and food to the same extent as Europeans and Asians. When information to the effect that Lascelles had suggested a war bonus for Africans leaked out,[2] ten clerks and interpreters, mainly from the office of the District Commissioner, Mengo, petitioned the Governor to rectify the situation. Yusufu Bamuta, Sulemani Waligo, and Yosamu Kubanja were among the petitioners who pointed out that the rise in prices had "spared no race or people" and that they had been taught by the missionaries as well as the Government to raise their standard of living, which they had done by consuming imported articles.[3]

---

[1] U.N.A.S.M.P. 5265/1, min. 12, memorandum from the C.S., 4.25.18.

[2] This was no small discovery because in those days African clerks were generally not permitted to see files, vote books, or to touch typewriters! This was stated by pioneer African clerks such as Paulo Kavuma and Y. K. Lubogo and confirmed by D. G. Tomblings, the Principal of Makerere College from 1925 to 1939.

[3] U.N.A.S.M.P. 6371, Clerks c/o D.C.'s office, Kampala (Kla.) to D. C. Mengo, 7.9.19 enc. in min. 2, P. C. Buganda to C.S., 7.17.19.

J. C. R. Sturrock, the Acting Provincial Commissioner for
Buganda, backed the petition commenting that those six African
clerks covered by the 1912 Regulations should be entitled to war
bonuses. The Treasurer, however, turned down the petition on the
grounds that special relief was unnecessary and inadvisable for
Africans and that "if they did receive any additional money they
would only squander it."[1]

In the same month, July 1919, a second petition with 25
signatures, including those of Serwano Kulubya, J. Kamulegeya and
Sepiriya Kadumukasa, was presented to the Chief Secretary.[2] This
time, non-clerical employees such as medical assistants and others
working in the various government offices at Kampala and Mengo
rallied behind the clerks thus displaying a new sense of solidarity. But the petition did not change the government stand on the
war bonus. The Governor ruled "that the cost of living for native
employees had not risen to such an extent as to warrant the grant
of a war bonus."[3] The dissatisfied and unyielding Africans collected 37 signatures in July 1920 and appealed that their case be
reviewed. Claiming to represent "all Native employees in the
Protectorate" they lamented:

> Now we find that if nothing is done for us towards our
> cost of living we shall be ruined. The Imported Non-
> European Government employees who are not British
> Subjects* ate receiving Government sympathy, whereas
> every consideration is denied to us who are British
> protected subjects.[4]

---

[1] Ibid., min. 4, Treasurer (C. K. Dain)to C. S., 7.28.19.
There is no record of the official reply to the petition.

[2] Ibid., min. 7, 25 African signatories to C. S., 7.29.19.

[3] Ibid., min. 18, Ag. C.S. to P.C., Buganda, 2.2.20.

[4] Ibid., min. 19, 37 African Government Servants to C.S.,
7.20.20.

* A reference to Goanese (Goans). Goa was a Portuguese
enclave in India until 1961.

The organizers of this petition had somehow learned that a war bonus had been approved for the African employees of the Kenya Government,[1] but this did not strengthen their case. Yusufu Bamuta and his 36 aggrieved friends were informed that no war bonus would be granted, but that the NCS, then under consideration, would probably remove their grievances.[2]

Despite its failure, this campaign for war bonuses by the educated Africans in government service would appear to be extremely significant. It gave rise to some measure of collective action and served as the nucleus from which one of the first intertribal associations--the future Uganda African Civil Servants' Association--grew in the 1920s. It also revealed that the new generations of mission-educated Africans were neither docile nor conformists but took easy offense at being excluded from the privileged colonial set-up. Moreover, the pattern for future activities of African civil servants in Uganda was established. Asian staff became a thorn in their flesh, and parity with Asians their ultimate objective.

Other African grievances stemmed from their vague and undefined status in the eyes of the Government. Their attempts to correct this situation revealed growing African confidence and resentment against racial discrimination and the employment of Asian clerks. Indeed the frustrations of ambitious and able African clerks in government service were so great that many asked to be transferred to the native authorities.

---

[1] Ibid. There is no evidence of any links between the petitioners and the "African Civil Service Association of the British East Africa Protectorate" in existence since 1919. See U.N.A.S.M.P. 5998, C. C. Bowring to Milner, 4.7.20. It is possible that Kamulegeya might have found this out from one of his contacts in Nairobi, or one of the clerks could have got the information from a sympathetic official. Future research into the totally unknown history of the African C.S.A. of the B.E.A. Protectorate and comparison with the activities of the BGNEA should further illuminate the nature of educated African protest in East Africa.

[2] U.N.A.S.M.P. 6371, min. 21, C.S. to Y. Bamuta and other signatories, 9.10.20.

A controversy had started over what African clerks and interpreters should wear. Almost all clerks and interpreters were graduates of mission schools where they had absorbed Christian ideas and had been exposed to some aspects of European civilization. They had been taught to abandon bark cloth and some of their tribal customs which were repugnant to Europeans, and they had been encouraged to practice many "civilized" customs. Their common desire was to learn English and absorb as much English culture as possible. (Watson, 1968) Knowledge of English was the passport to enter the clerical and allied posts; and both Africans and Asians considered the imitation of Europeans as natural and desirable, since Europeans constituted the ruling and privileged class. The Budo Old Boys' Club (BOBC)--most of whose members were government clerks and interpreters or chiefs--requested a ruling from the Provincial Commissioner, Buganda, on what clothes they should wear while on duty. Some of its members had been dismissed from government employment for wearing suits, ties or hats. Their superior officers wanted them to wear either Khanzus or trousers--Khanzu-coat combinations without ties or hats.[1] The Provincial Commissioner advised the members of the BOBC to wear whatever their heads of offices required them to wear.[2] The Secretariat had given a similar ruling to the African interpreter Ernesti Sebagala who had complained about the high-handedness of the District Commicsioner, Entebbe, who had forced him to wear a Khanzu at work.[3]

Educated Africans were mortified by such British attitudes towards them. Sebagala and the Old Budonians could not fathom why Africans could not wear what they chose as did the other groups.

---

[1] Buganda, M.P. no. 1447, min. 46, BOBC to P.C., Buganda, 3.6.22. Khanzu is a full-length, long-sleeved, collarless white robe introduced by the Arabs and Swahilis; it was adopted by many of the chiefs as their uniform. Now it is widely worn in Uganda, especially in the rural areas by the peasantry.

[2] Ibid., min. 46A, Sturrock to Vice President BOBC, 3.25.22.

[3] U.N.A.S.M.P. 5480, min. 4, Ag. C.S. to E. Sebagala; u.f.s. D.C., Entebbe (Ebb.), 10.16.18.

Sebagala, in fact, had presented a breakdown of his personal expenses to show that it was more economical for him to wear a suit than a Khanzu. Having pointed out that the Khanzu was as foreign as European clothes to Buganda, he assured his superiors that he was not "trying to be a European" by wearing a suit.[1]

It would appear that the British officers sent out to the colonies were neither enthusiastic nor indiscriminate Anglicizers. Through Christianity, education and contact with Europeans, they hoped to strengthen the moral qualities of the subject peoples, "discipline" them and harmonize their habits of work to the practices of industrialized European societies. Natives who displayed merely the external trappings of Western civilization, such as clothes, were, in general, frowned upon. Unlike the French, who did not hesitate to make Frenchmen out of the small African elites in the colonies, the British did not favor the growth of a class of black Englishmen. It has been suggested that the men of the Colonial Service, with their upper middle-class, public school background, who remained "apart and above" the lower classes in England, "became even more culturally rigid abroad." (Heussler, 1963; Symonds, 1966)

British officials in Uganda, especially after the 1914-1918 war, desired to preserve tribal institutions and encourage educated Africans to apply their knowledge to improving the conditions of their own people. Native Governments were considered to be the rightful place for the majority of talented Africans. Thus, identifying Africans with their tribal governments seemed to be linked to the question of requiring them to wear Khanzu and coat--which had become the uniform of most chiefs in Uganda. Wearing European clothes was on the ascendancy among clerks and chiefs. Sturrock realized that much as this tendency should be deprecated, it could only be staved off and never stopped, causing serious problems in the meantime. He advocated a general policy of letting Africans wear what they liked as long as it was decent, "neat and

---

[1] Ibid., min. 1, Sebagala to C.S., 10.8.18.

unostentatious."[1] His policy was supported by his colleagues and the European costumes controversy was short-lived.

The 38 Africans who, led by Bamuta and Erasito Bakaluba, had previously campaigned for war bonuses, renewed their demands in 1922. Juxtaposing their own ability with that of the Goans, they found little difference between their relative merits. They reminded the Government that many departments and offices could not carry on without African interpreters and assistants; they were needed as much as Goan clerks. Yet, they lamented that while the Government made a fetish of Goan clerks, Africans were not "appreciated at all" and their pay was "far too inadequate." No attempts were made to disguise their bitterness towards either the Protectorate Government or its protégès, the Goan clerks:

> The only work that is given any consideration is that of Goanese clerks and no matter how inexperienced these Goanese may be.
>
> We shall be much obliged if the Government were to recognize our work and that every chance given to Natives who show abilities to start filling up positions now occupied by these alien clerks who are debarring us from getting any appointment of any importance in our own country.

Clearly, the African employees felt that they were not getting their due. Asian clerks were elevated well above African clerks; the Goans, in particular, were treated as the brahmins of the clerical service whereas the Africans were made to feel like outcasts. It is doubtful whether all the clerks among these men really thought that they were as experienced as their Goan counterparts who had the advantages of better education and a long tradition of clerical work. However, it is significant that under the leadership of courageous clerks like Bamuta and Bakaluba, who were ready to criticize the Protectorate Government in no uncertain terms, African employees had begun to cooperate with each other. They

---

[1] Ankole District Archives, Mbarara, (A.D.A.) M.P. no. 57, ADM., min. 22, Sturrock, P.C., Buganda, to P.C.W.P., P.C.E.P., and P.C.N.P., 10.5.22.

concluded their letter of complaint by inquiring about the expected date of the introduction of the NCS which, they had been told, would remove many of their grievances.[1]

Formation of the British Government Native Employees Association (BGNEA)

The petition-writing during the past three years had generated some degree of unity among the skilled African employees working in the government offices at Kampala, Mengo and Entebbe. They had joined hands on one or two issues which were likely to benefit all of them. These loose threads of cooperation were woven into a single, formal association, at the end of 1922. Erasito Bakalube, the Head Interpreter in the office of the District Commissioner, Entebbe, was elected president of the newly formed "Native Civil Servants Association."[2] This association was formed to promote the general interests of natives in government service and it had no connections with chiefs in the Kabaka's Government. Bakaluba seems to have emphasized this separate identity of the members of his association so that they might not be treated in the same way as chiefs in the Native Governments but as Protectorate officials, since European and Asian officials of the British Government in Uganda were granted many privileges. Perhaps by identifying themselves with the Protectorate Government, the native employees hoped to share some of the privileges enjoyed by non-European employees.

However, the Native Civil Servants Association (NCSA) was unable to obtain official recognition under that name. E. L. Scott, the Assistant Secretary for Native Affairs, in consultation with Sturrock, decided not to recognize a body calling itself the

---

[1] U.N.A.S.M.P. 6371, min. 22, 38 African employees, Ebb., to C.S. 1.7.22.

[2] U.N.A.S.M.P. 7673, min. 1, E. Bakaluba to C.S., 12.28.22. Among the founder members were Y. Bamuta, Michaeri Kintu and Simon Muwanjuzi from the D.C.'s Office, Entebbe; P. N. Kavuma, P.C.'s Office, Kampala and E. Lule from the Post Office, Kampala. Apparently all the 38 Africans who had signed the petition of 1.7.22 joined the association.

NCSA when "many of its members may possibly not be admitted to the Native Civil Service on its institution."[1] Bakaluba replied that since none of the Africans knew what the NCS regulations would be like, they wanted to be recognized as a group without necessarily being connected to the NCS.[2] When this proposal was rejected, Bakaluba requested a meeting between an African deputation from his association and the Governor.[3] Scott, however, scornfully dismissed the idea:

> These youths should not as yet be recognised in a corporate capacity. They should be informed that if any individual considers that he has a grievance, he can put the matter forward to the Governor through the head of his department.

The Chief Secretary endorsed this viewpoint, but the Governor felt that he had a much better understanding of native psychology than his Secretary entrusted with the conduct of native affairs:

> My own view, as a result of long and close experience of natives, is that it would be best for the Secretary of Native Affairs to interview these young men. It will give them an opportunity to air any grievance, real or imaginary, that they may have; it will give the Secretary of Native Affairs an opportunity of showing he is closely interested in their affairs and welfare. If there is anything wrong, it will be put right. And they will go away having had their say and got their troubles off their chests perfectly happy and contented! You can't stop these organizations-- the thing to do is to [discourage?] them, and show them that they have no real grievance.[4]

The wiser counsel of the Governor prevailed. Bakaluba was asked to meet the Secretary for Native Affairs, with four other

---

[1] U.N.A.S.M.P. 7673, min. 3, Scott to Bakaluba, 1.10.23.

[2] Ibid., min. 4, Bakaluba to C.S., 4.3.23.

[3] Ibid., min. 6, Bakaluba to Governor, 4.18.23.

[4] Ibid., min. 9, Archer (Governor) to C.S., 4.30.23.

native employees from different offices. At this meeting on
May 25, 1923, the African employees were, for the first time,
acquainted with some details of the NCS scheme. The African deputation also renewed the question of government recognition of the
NCSA. Since they had been previously informed that the difficulties preventing the Government from recognizing their association
were essentially semantic, they came up with a new name: the
"British Government Native Employees' Association" (BGNEA). This
clever maneuver, however, did not impress the Secretary for Native
Affairs. He was still unconvinced about the judiciousness of
encouraging such associations "in a race still in its infancy."
But he grudgingly withdrew his objection on the grounds that "discontent will always organise itself in some way in an intelligent
race, and it is better to have an open recognised organisation
than perhaps a secret unrecognised one."[1]

It is significant that although all the founding members
of this association were Baganda they did not adopt a tribal name.
Instead, they chose "native" to represent and signify their distinct identity. They realized that they were different from the
Europeans and the Asians. "Native" was interpreted as meaning the
true sons of the soil, the indigenous people. Its derogatory connotation does not seem to have aroused African sensibilities at
that time.[2] Also, under this name, non-Baganda African civil
servants would more readily seek membership in the future. The
formation of the BGNEA preceded the introduction of the NCS and it
was conceived as a pressure group to ameliorate the conditions of
service of its members. The BGNEA soon began to assert itself,
taking up complaints of various kinds. Some Government Offices in
Entebbe, especially the Land Office, were reported to be notorious
for their severity on African staff.[3] The Land Office did not

---

[1] Ibid., min. 13, Scott to Jarvis, 5.25.23.

[2] I am grateful to Mr. P. N. Kavuma (interview, Kampala, 2.26.70) and Mr. A. L. Kagobya (interview, Kampala, 7.8.70) for enlightening me on this aspect of the BGNEA's history.

[3] Public Works Department and the Veterinary and Agricultural Offices in Entebbe were also in the black books of Africans. Interviews: Kavuma, 2.26.70; Lubogo, 5.15.70; E. M. K. Mulira, 2.22.70.

permit its African staff to wear shoes on its premises. The most satisfactory answer the African staff could get from the Land Office on this subject was that they should "not forget their grandfathers' Native Customs."[1] Since most government offices did not prohibit their African employees from wearing shoes, the BGNEA implored that this anomaly be set right. The Acting Assistant Secretary for Native Affairs assured the BGNEA that the Land Office did not intend to cast a slur on its African staff. It was simply a necessary measure "to minimise the noise which on stone or cement floors is inevitable if shoes or boots are worn."[2]

Housing for Africans was another major grievance. Yusufu Bamuta, who was occupying a government house in Entebbe, was evicted to make room for a non-African employee. Bamuta promptly claimed a housing allowance and this stirred up a controversy in government circles. Hitherto Blasio Kagwa was the only African who had been paid a housing allowance. The Labour Commissioner held that Bamuta would have to be paid this allowance since he was entitled to it under the 1912 Regulations. But he warned that in doing so an undesirable precedent could be created. Therefore, he suggested amending the 1912 Regulations so as to deny this privilege to Africans covered by them.[3] Since the legal opinion felt that the Government was bound to pay such an allowance under the 1912 Regulations,[4] the Executive Council advised that Bamuta's claims should be settled in his favor, but that a government

---

[1] U.N.A.S.M.P. 5480, min. 15, Bakaluba to C.S., 9.19.23.

[2] Ibid., min. 16, Ag. A.S.N.A. to Bakaluba, 10.19.23. Cf. Kulubya's reply regarding the use of shoes and boots by Ugandan Africans before the Joint Committee of both Houses on Closer Union in East Africa, London, May 12, 1931, reproduced in D. A. Low, The Mind of Buganda, London, 1971, p. 96.

[3] U.N.A.S.M.P. 7582, min. 3, Scott to C.S., 1.5.22. One suspects that Bamuta, with his English education and as Apolo Kagwa's son-in-law, felt that his case was also exceptional and seems to have resented being treated just like any other African employee. B. Kagwa was the Katikiro's (Chief Minister) English-educated son.

[4] Ibid., min. 7, Attorney-General to C.S., 1.28.22.

circular should be issued immediately disqualifying all other natives in the future.[1]

The Government's continued delay in settling Bamuta's case provoked the BGNEA to accuse the Government of practicing racial discrimination. The official reply that only Africans serving outside their tribal areas would be given housing allowances did not satisfy the BGNEA. It played the last card it had in its hand by requesting an interview with the Governor, but to no avail.[2] Though the effectiveness of the BGNEA was limited, African employees were at least able to make their individual and collective difficulties known to the proper authorities with far greater confidence than ever before.

The BGNEA also questioned the Government on the rights of government officers in terminating appointments. E. Lwanga, a clerk in the Land Office, had been dismissed without notice for incompetence. The BGNEA condemned this:

> While we quite realise the right of any employer to engage or discharge anyone as his work demands, we strongly deprecate any such action as an immediate discharge...

This letter which protested and preached at the same time concluded with a definite call for an urgent end to all such abuse of power against African staff.[3] This was a challenge to the heads of departments and other officer "hire and fire at will" practices. The Government noted the force and fairness of the BGNEA's argument but explained that in Lwanga's case no injustice had been done.[4] This was a step forward in the struggle for better conditions of service. Indeed, the activities of the BGNEA during the first few years after its inception were quite astonishing. Most of the members were low-paid and extremely vulnerable employees,

---

[1] Ibid., min. 8, Excerpts, Executive Council meeting, 2.22.22.

[2] U.N.A.S.M.P. 7913, min. 5, Bakaluba to A.S.N.A., 1.24.24.

[3] U.N.A.S.M.P. 5533, min. 50, Bakaluba to C.S., 9.8.24.

[4] Ibid., min. 53, A.S.N.A. to the Secretary, BGNEA, 10.17.24.

not yet enjoying any official protection against dismissal or victimization.[1]

The BGNEA, however, failed to extend its activities from the field of protest to that of self-improvement. In Tanganyika, Martin Kayamba had founded the Tanganyika Territory African Civil Service Association (TTACSA) in March 1922. As Iliffe has commented: "This was designed as the first of many civil servants' clubs which were to be formed throughout the country. They would help their members improve themselves by opening libraries, buying newspapers, and teaching English." (Iliffe, 1969) There was no parallel undertaking in Uganda. English lessons or tuition in the practical side of clerical work from the more experienced members of the BGNEA could have helped a greater number of African clerks to feel more at home in the government offices.[2] Nevertheless, the BGNEA seems to have been a dynamic and successful organization.

The future effectiveness as well as the characteristics of the BGNEA and the NCS were to be affected by a certain pattern in the British approach to native administration. It has been seen that, between 1919 and 1922, the African staff in the Protectorate Administration had found leaders like Kamulegeya, Bamuta, and Bakaluba who forcefully but respectfully asserted African rights. Moreover, being among the very few efficient African clerks and interpreters then available in Uganda, they were in quite a favorable position vis-a-vis the Government. However, instead of these and other educated Africans becoming the core of a future African civil service, their number shrank. This was largely as a result of their transfer to the native governments to take up chieftaincies. To cite a few cases: Sepiriya Kadumukasa was appointed a

---

[1] A. L. Kagobya, President of the BGNEA from 1935-1945, conveyed that some government offices threatened their employees with dismissal if they actively supported the association. He contends that the Land Office continued to prohibit its African employees from wearing shoes up to 1925, in order to persuade them to resign from the BGNEA (Interview, 7.8.70).

[2] Until 1929 there was no other effective way of learning clerical work.

gombolola (sub-county) chief in Kyadondo county in 1919; Sulemani Waligo filled a similar vacancy in 1921; Bamuta was seconded to the Kabaka's Government in 1924 as Secretary to the Lukiko (Royal Assembly). From the 1920s onwards, many clerks and interpreters like Kamulegeya, Bakaluba, Petero Serumaga, Serwanga K. Sadulaka, Yosiya Sewali, Joseph Bampade, Michaeri Kintu and many others trod in the footsteps of the earlier clerks.

The "odd man out" was Yosamu Kubanja, who resigned from the Government to take up employment with a Kampala commercial firm which offered him a higher salary. It was not by a series of accidents that so few educated Africans remained in government service. From about the 1920s, the Protectorate Government had embarked on a course of greater control over and increased bureaucratization of the native administrations. Government officials interfered in native administrations more frequently than before to prevent what they thought to be abuses, corruption and injustices to the peasantry. Hence the policy of retiring inefficient or undesirable chiefs in Buganda and the removal of Baganda chiefs serving outside Buganda. (Low & Pratt, 1960; Twaddle, 1969; Low, 1971) The British officials in Uganda were in search of a new breed of better educated collaborators. Government offices had thus become breeding places for future chiefs. Mission-trained youths employed as clerks or interpreters would come under European observation. Habits of punctuality, probity, perseverance and sobriety would be reinforced and spread into their tribal governments. At this time, educated Africans also preferred to serve as chiefs. In the 1920s the vast majority of them were Baganda. The Kagwas and the Kulubyas were useful to the Protectorate Government, but they were needed even more by the Kabaka's Government. Moreover, the continued employment of ambitious or meritorious Africans in sedentary work in the Protectorate Government was not without its peculiar problems because the Civil Service had acquired racial characteristics which generally confined Africans to the lower grades. It seemed a sensible practice to divert ambitious or competent clerks and interpreters to the native authorities where they could rise to the highest ranks, rather than retain them in the central superstructure where they were bound to become discontented. This diversion of educated Africans to the tribal governments served two purposes: making tribal governments more efficient as well as pacifying the African elite.

Creation of the NCS

By December 1924, the revised NCS proposals, acceptable to London and Entebbe, had been hammered out. However, the NCSC had to bow down to London on housing, leave, automatic annual salary increments, and, above all, pensions. To all intents and purposes, the NCS had turned out to be, not a pensionable service open to the majority of employees, as originally planned, but a drastically restricted pensionable establishment, to which only Makerere-educated men would be admitted.[1]

It was to be governed by the NCS Regulations of 1924 (the 1924 Regulations). For the bulk of the Africans who would be denied admission to the pensionable NCS, separate regulations--the Native Employees Regulations of 1925 (the 1925 Regulations) had to be introduced. Their terms of service were as similar as possible to those of the NCS, except that there were no provisions for pensions or gratuities; instead a bonus was to be granted on retirement.[2] The African staff was now officially divided into two sections: the pensionable Native Civil Servants controlled by the 1924 Regulations, and the non-pensionable employees controlled by the 1925 Regulations. All Africans not appointed to the NCS were automatically eligible for service under the 1925 Regulations. Both sets of the above regulations were translated into Luganda by Serwano Kulubya and were subsequently published together with the English version.[3] As far as the Protectorate Government was concerned, the NCS could now be activated in 1925.

---

[1] Makerere College, started in 1921-22, was then a government technical school to provide the technical departments with subordinate African staff.

[2] U.N.A.S.M.P. 8306, min. 12, Governor to S. of S., 11.21.24.

[3] Ibid., min. 14, Sturrock to Asst. C.S., 12.8.24.

African Boycott of the NCS

The African staff, however, viewed the situation differently. The BGNEA advised its members to dissociate themselves from both the <u>1924 Regulations</u> and the <u>1925 Regulations</u>.[1] The much-experienced Erasito Bakaluba and Yusufu Bamuta, who had led the BGNEA since its inception in December 1922, were no longer in the service of the Protectorate Government, both having taken up much more important positions in the Buganda Government.[2] This "brain-drain" from the Protectorate Government to the Native Administrations became more apparent in the 1920s. It would tend to reduce the effectiveness of the BGNEA and jeopardize the future prospects of the NCS. The burden of conducting the negotiations with the Protectorate Government fell upon Petero Serumaga, a Muganda clerk in the Secretariat, and Zakayo Waswa who were the BGNEA's president and secretary, respectively.

At its meeting on May 12, 1925, the BGNEA scrutinized the two sets of regulations affecting the African staff and in July sent the Government several observations. The African employees, who had not been consulted in framing the regulations, were very disappointed. Rejecting both the grading of the posts and the salary increment scales which were described as "very poor," the BGNEA stated that it was greatly perturbed by the omission of free housing in the Regulations. The question of housing had manifold implications for the Africans and it remained unsolved for a long time. The BGNEA further represented that its members preferred two months leave every three years to 14 days leave each year.

The 30 year service in a pensionable office in order to qualify for a pension, also seemed "scarcely attainable." The BGNEA wondered how a native, who had spent the best part of his working age in government service prior to the institution of the NCS could possibly serve for another 30 years so as to earn his

---

[1] U.N.A.S.M.P. 8819, BGNEA to C.S., 7.17.25.

[2] Bamuta had been appointed Secretary to the Lukiko in 1924. Bakaluba had become an Accounts Clerk with the Lukiko in 1925.

pension. Therefore, it implored that the services rendered by such natives to the Government, prior to their admission to the NCS, should be taken into account when calculating pensions or gratuities. As for the plight of the vast majority of the native staff--who would not be admitted to the NCS--it was strongly pleaded that their pay, leave, housing and general conditions of employment should be sympathetically reconsidered.[1]

This protest to the Government seems to have been followed by a general notice from the BGNEA's Entebbe headquarters to all its branches to boycott the NCS.[2] Though at present it is impossible to estimate the approximate number and strength of the branches of the BGNEA, it has been stated, from memory, by some of the more recent officials of the successor to this association, that they existed at almost every District Commissioner's Office since the mid-twenties.[3] The Native Civil Service Board (NCSB), also created in 1924, discussed the BGNEA's representations and communicated its views through E. B. Jarvis, the Chief Secretary.

Jarvis informed Petero Serumaga that "the average standard of efficiency and reliability among native employees" was "very low." The Secretariat did not think that there were more than "half a dozen" native clerks in government service who had a good command of English. Jarvis emphasized the poorness of the majority of the native clerks at filing correspondence correctly, at keeping accounts and generally in performing office-related duties. However, he conceded that improper and inadequate training methods and a weak educational background were partly responsible for some

---

[1] C.O. 536/146/14243, BGNEA to C.S., 7.17.25.

[2] A.D.A., File No. STF/149, min. 11, BGNEA, Mbarara Branch to D.C., Ankole; cc, BGNEA, Entebbe, 12.30.25. The nine Africans in the D.C.'s office who signed this letter were mostly Baganda clerks and interpreters.

[3] Interviews, 1970: Kavuma, Kagobya, S.B.K. Musoke, P. Semakula. Attempts to locate the files and other documents of the BGNEA have so far failed. Perhaps a thorough examination of all the District Archives of Uganda will throw more light on the activities and importance of what seems to be a most fascinating but least known African protest group of the 1920s.

of these shortcomings:

> With the improved educational facilities which the Government are now gradually introducing, a higher standard of education and efficiency may be expected in the future with a corresponding rise in salaries.

On the whole, the Government showed no intention of yielding to the African demands. Automatic annual salary increments were refused; each case would be considered on its own merits. The request for free quarters was turned down but with an assurance that all deserving cases would be considered favorably--if and when funds permitted. Finally, Jarvis promised that the Government would consult the Colonial Office as to whether or not the previous service of those Africans admitted to the NCS should be considered when computing pensions and gratuities.[1]

This first exchange of opposing views on the NCS soon degenerated into protracted verbal warfare between the Protectorate Government and some of its African staff. The main cause of this dispute was the paternalistic and somewhat unsympathetic governmental attitude towards its African personnel. The dissatisfied BGNEA appealed to the Chief Secretary to reconsider this decision and to bring the entire matter before the Governor. In its retort to the Chief Secretary's rather uncompromising words about the native clerks, the BGNEA complained that it was unfair of the Government to brand all the native employees as inefficient and unreliable by singling out the weaknesses of clerks and ignoring the good work of native artisans, medical assistants, drivers and other skilled personnel. It also expressed regret that the Government had completely overlooked the large economies achieved, through the employment of Africans instead of Asians, in many of the subordinate technical and professional branches of the public services.

Regarding the admittedly lamentable quality of some African clerks, Waswa replied that this should hardly have aroused government comment. He reminded the Government that the more able and

---

[1] U.N.A.S.M.P. 8819, min. 6, C.S. to President, BGNEA, 2.20.26.

outstanding African clerks were continually lost to private firms and the native administrations. The crux of the matter was, as Waswa put it, that "the native employee has no real prospects in the Government Service..." This, indeed, was the fountain of the many obstacles which bedevilled the development of the NCS.

Housing was yet another thorny problem which tended to lessen the popularity of government service among many educated Africans. The BGNEA strove laboriously to convince the Government that great hardships had been heaped upon the Africans with the collapse of some of the tribal customs in the realm of hospitality (to strangers). The frustrations and the exasperations of many Baganda employees in finding accommodation when they were transferred from their own locality to another part of their tribal territory were outlined at some length. The petition ended by bseeeching the Governor to alleviate the sufferings of the African staff, particularly in matters related to housing, since the "old, friendly, and generous African hospitality had vanished with the advent of modern ideas; and again this attitude is most pronounced in Government Stations."[1]

By the end of 1925 housing for the African staff had already become a burning question, affecting several categories of employees in different departments. The NCSB pondered over this problem and came out in favor of providing quarters for "the higher grade of native staff" in all government stations even in their own tribal areas.[2] Likewise, Governor Gowers had made a special concession in the case of artisans employed by the Public Works Department. The persistent shortage of artisans had considerably hampered major government building and construction projects. Maximum productivity through improved efficiency and greater punctuality among the native artisans employed by the Public Works Department seemed to be the most practicable, immediate answer. This could only be attained by providing quarters

---

[1] C.O. 536/146/14243, BGNEA to the Governor, 4.27.26, enclosed in Waswa to C.S., 4.28.26.

[2] U.N.A.S.M.P. 7913, min. 32, Excerpts, NCSB Minutes, 11.4.25.

near the workshops and the construction sites and by supplementing the plantain-oriented diet of the Baganda with free rations of grain and proteins.[1]

In 1927 the Executive Council approved the provision of government housing for native telegraphists but overruled the NCSB's wishes to extend free lodgings to all the skilled native personnel. Only native telegraphists and artisans were given government housing since they constituted special cases. Otherwise, the official position remained unchanged as revealed by the Governor's minute on the African petition: "I certainly don't want to extend the principle of free quarters. If we provide quarters for native staff, they should pay rent."

The government reply to the BGNEA's petition was noncommittal and African clerks as well as artisans were again criticized. The Chief Secretary, however, did mention the possibility of providing accommodation in individual cases on the recommendation of the Heads of Departments. Jarvis ended on a consolatory note by informing the BGNEA that civil servants in Britain did not qualify for free housing or allowances in lieu, when serving on local terms.[2]

The BGNEA, however, was far from consoled; on the contrary it pursued the dispute even further. Waswa requested the Chief Secretary to forward another petition, together with copies of all previous correspondence between his association and the Protectorate Government, to the Secretary of State for the Colonies. Implicit in their desire to bring the matter before the highest authorities in London would appear to be a deep-seated suspicion among many of the officials of the BGNEA that the Protectorate Government had not been fair to the Africans.[3]

---

[1] C.O. 536/137, W.F. Gowers to S. of S., 11.9.25. The C.O. had flatly refused permission to import 100 Indian artisans. Hence the necessity to offer better working conditions to the African artisans.

[2] U.N.A.S.M.P. 8819, min. 12, Jarvis to Secretary, BGNEA, 6.1.26.

[3] Ibid., min. 13. In the absence of any other records of the BGNEA, the writer has accepted P.N. Kavuma's (a pioneer member

It was politely but firmly restated in their supplication that the Protectorate Government must assume the responsibility for housing its African staff, just as it did in the case of its non-African staff. This central point was amplified, both to remind the Scretary of State about the great diversity in the socio-economic conditions of Uganda and Britain and to invalidate the Entebbe officials' stand that the Uganda Africans should not grumble about housing because their counterparts in the British Civil Service did not do so:

> ...This country differs very widely from other more civilized countries where a person could obtain lodgings by hiring them...no person, whether native or not, would hold a post contentedly while always in the fear that he is liable at every moment to be moved, but never sure as to whether he will be able to get reasonable quarters; and in the case of married persons, the position is felt the more acute.

African salary scales had also been causing considerable anguish. The petitioners entreated the Secretary of State to see that the native employees were adequately remunerated "to meet the increased cost of native living."[1]

In an age when African dignitaries like Apolo Kagwa could be dismissed (Low & Pratt, 1960), and native kings could be threatened with deposition for being impolite to British government officials,[2] the toughness and the boldness of these ordinary African youths is quite astonishing. They showed remarkable awareness (for that period and with the educational restrictions

---

of the association since the 1920s) explanation for this and subsequent petitions to the S. of S. "The Baganda were always suspicious of everything the British did," remarked Tomblings (interview, 5.30.70). Cf. Apolo Kagwa's Personal Petition to the S. of S., 3.30.26, reproduced as document 25 in Low, Mind, op. cit., pp. 70-73; E.M.K. Mulira, Troubled Uganda, Fabian Pamphlet, 1950, pp. 16-22.

[1] C.O. 536/146/14243, BGNEA to S. of S., 1.18.27, enclosed in Governor to S. of S., 8.5.27.

[2] Daudi Kasagama, the Omukama (king) of Toro had read "an offensive letter" to him from Cooper (P.C.W.P.) before a public meeting. The Executive Council recommended "that the Mukama should be instructed to appear at Entebbe...failing a satisfactory

upon Africans) (Motani, 1976) of wider problems and their own third-class status in the Civil Service.

The Governor did not transmit the African petition to the Colonial Office for seven months. The delay was attributed to the reconstitution of the NCSB which later held long discussions on the issues raised by the BGNEA. As before, the reconstituted NCSB comprised European officials only. When Gowers did transmit the petition in August 1927 he forewarned the Colonial Office not to become so sentimental over reading what the Uganda natives had to say. Gowers stressed in his dispatch accompanying the petition that while the Uganda Government was not blind to the special cases of hardships among its African employees, it had decided against extending the principle of free accommodation to the Africans as a whole.[1]

Though the Colonial Office was impressed by the terse and effective manner in which the BGNEA had made its points, it fully endorsed the Governor's policy. The responsibility and the decision-making powers pertinent to the NCS were delegated to the Governor. He was further authorized to devise, with the help of the NCSB, the necessary measures to settle the outstanding questions such as the computing of pensions and whether or not to consider the services of the native employees rendered prior to their admission to the NCS for this purpose. Thus, in short, Entebbe now had a free hand to develop the NCS within the broad framework already approved by London in 1925. The destiny of the NCS would now be shaped largely by the outlook of the Entebbe officials.[2]

---

explanation the Mukama should be suspended or deposed." See C.O., 685/25, Exco minutes, 3.8.26 and 3.27.26.

[1] C.O. 536/146/14243, Governor to S. of S., 8.5.27.

[2] Ibid., C.O. to Gowers, 9.28.27. In 1928 the C.O. laid down that all matters regarding pensions and gratuities for the non-European staff could be resolved locally. It was no longer necessary to consult the S. of S. if specific regulations already existed for these purposes. See U.N.A.S.M.P. 2802/B, min. 73, S. of S. (Amery) to Governor, 4.28.28. By this time, the Treasury had also relaxed its grip over colonial budgets, if the dependencies were self-sufficient.

R. Rankine, who had succeeded Jarvis as Chief Secretary in 1927, informed the BGNEA that its petition had been reviewed by the Secretary of State, and that he had concurred with the Protectorate Government's opinion in the dispute. Though free government housing for the African personnel once again had been categorically rejected, individual applications, it was promised, would be received with compassion. But Rankine clarified that when the Government felt the necessity to provide quarters for any category of the African employees, a rent would be charged.[1]

---

[1] U.N.A.S.M.P. 8819, min. 22, C.S. to BGNEA, 12.12.27. The housing issue needs further consideration here on account of its wider consequences for the African employees. Government accommodation for them being severely restricted, most of the African staff lived in their village homes. The indifferent location of African lodgings generated some disquieting problems which complicated their lives as public servants. Living anywhere between two miles and twenty miles away from the government offices, commuting to and from them was a difficult matter. Low wages precluded widespread possession of bicycles thus compelling the greater number of Africans to walk to work. It was not uncommon for many Africans to rise at 4 a.m. or 5 a.m. in order to reach the centers of employment, punctually, and to pass the whole day without eating any food. The pressing need to return home before darkness did not enable African staff to establish any informal social contact with European and Asian civil servants and they continued to live in their different worlds generally ignorant of each other's problems and ways of life.

To fulfill two opposite roles--that of acceptable members of the village communities in which they lived among the peasantry and that of good public servants in the departments where they worked--was a trying task. Traditional beer parties and daily drinking bouts gathered momentum at night and went on until the small hours. Intemperate drinking had assumed epidemic proportions during the early 1920s, the principal offenders being chiefs and the salaried educated Africans. Investigations conducted by the four Provincial Commissioners in 1920 uncovered a few alarming facts. It was reported that "the materials from which fermented liquor is made are an irreplaceable element of normal diet" of the people outside Buganda. The District Commissioners for Ankole and Bunyoro pointed out that in their areas beer itself made up a necessary item of food. Five years later the Governor painted a dismal picture of habitual drunkenness in Uganda, attributing this to a situation wherein the staple food and the ingredients for manufacturing beer were the same. Fruits and grains used in brewing, being essential parts of the tribal nourishment, "are found in every garden, and an expert knowledge of their use for this purpose is a necessary qualification of every housewife. Every hut is

For its part, the BGNEA terminated its negotiations with the Protectorate Government on a melancholy note:

> In closing this correspondence I am desired to state that my association can only rely on the sympathy of the Government promised in the correspondence terminating with your letter under reply as otherwise the present position, as it affects the native employee, appears to them to be far from satisfactory.[1]

Repeated African entreaties had secured no concrete concessions regarding housing or salaries. It is hard to say whether the BGNEA could then have done anything else but leave the matter to government goodwill. There were apparently no precedents in Uganda of strikes involving civil servants.

BGNEA On The Offensive

Discontent among many of the African employees was bred by both mental and physical discomfort while in government employment. In large organizations such as the public services or the armed forces, discontent in any section of the personnel, whether caused by conditions of service, the work itself, or the unsympathetic attitude of superior officers, often leads to low morale and decline

---

therefore a potential brewery, with its material ready to hand," Gowers observed.

In the tribal societies there was no need to toil regularly six days a week, or to consume alcohol only at weekends or after office hours. Every day was a kind of a Sunday with a marked preference for leisure. Though such pastimes did not interfere with the village life of the peasantry, they seriously affected the performance of those village residents who also happened to be wage earners in the public services or in the competitive cash economy. Unregulated drinking and sleeping habits probably caused personal deterioration, unreliability, peevishness and strained relations with both colleagues and superiors at work. Addiction to intoxicants imposed extra pecuniary stresses. It sometimes led to borrowing or stealing of office funds or private indebtedness which wrecked many African careers. Most of the disciplinary actions against African civil servants taken by the NCSB and its successor, the African Civil Service Board (ACSB) were related to unpunctuality, lack of integrity in money matters and drunkenness. See Nizar Motani, thesis, op. cit., pp. 202-204.

[1] Ibid., min. 23, BGNEA to C.S., 2.3.28.

in efficiency. (Adu, 1965) Inefficiency and low morale seem to have become characteristic of this branch of the Protectorate Service comprising educated but disgruntled Africans.[1]

By 1928, however, the boycott of the NCS, initiated by the BGNEA and subsequently assisted by the negative attitude of the Uganda Government, had largely succeeded. Only five Africans had found their way into the NCS by April 1928.[2] Though the vast majority of the African employees, both skilled and unskilled, had not yet benefitted from the NCS, they had begun to display a new sense of awareness. Individual and collective complaints against the maltreatment of Africans by government officers were pouring into the Secretariat. The various letters in English and the vernaculars came from the highest as well as the most menial African employees and were levelled at European as well as non-European officers.[3]

Samwili Katiko and Eria, the two office messengers from the Public Works Department and the Audit Office, respectively, took up the plight of all their "Associates" in the government offices in 1925. Describing themselves as a part of the "responsible section of the Government Service," they begged of the Government not to exclude them from the privileges likely to be extended to other Africans in the Civil Service. Their accusations against the arbitrary dismissals suffered at the hands of Asian clerks and their dissatisfaction with the Government for being denied access to European officers, in order to present their grievances before them, indicated a kind of courage the like of which had not been generally seen before among most Africans.[4]

---

[1] "Educated" in this paper means those men with elementary and vocational training then available in Uganda.

[2] The Uganda Gazette, 4.30.28.

[3] At the U.N.A. the catalogue shows three files (SMP 5533, 5533/A and 5533/B) under the heading: "Natives-Complaints Against Government Officers and Servants." However, only SMP 5533 has survived; the other two are "missing."

[4] U.N.A.S.M.P. 6257, min. 46, S, Katiko and Eria to C.S., 6.8.25.

The Government, too, attempted to explain its own policies and difficulties to its office messengers rather than just ignore or dismiss their complaints. However, it was made abundantly clear to them that the European officers had more important matters to attend to and that office messengers would have to adjust themselves to the existing office methods. The Secretariat reply further stressed: "Good messengers who work well and get on well with the Asiatic clerks will probably receive increase of pay, others will not."[1]

At higher levels, clerks, interpreters, storekeepers and others who had been wronged by European or Asian staff and had failed to get a sympathetic hearing from their Heads of Departments bravely wrote to the Chief Secretary to intervene. More importantly, they often succeeded in getting investigations into their cases started on the direction of the Secretariat.[2]

The BGNEA also continued to pursue vigorously its members' cases with the same skill that it had demonstrated in trying to get the NCS scheme amended. The outstanding example was that of Mikairi Ntwanga, the Native Forester who had been summarily dismissed by Fyffe, the Conservator of Forests, when he requested to be spared his sixth transfer in six years at a time when African employees were not entitled to government housing. This had entailed great sufferings including living on the verandahs of the

---

[1] Ibid., min. 48, E.L. Scott (for C.S.) to S mwili Katiko, 7.3.25.

[2] U.N.A.S.M.P. 5533, passim. Especially see min. 54, J. Mitala, Native Clerk and Interpreter, D.C.'s office Tororo, to C.S., 3.12.26. Mitala revealed that the Medical Officer, Dr. Lee, had attempted to strike him with a stick simply because he was an African and that he had escaped injury only because he could run faster than Dr. Lee. An investigation was opened at the Secretariat's request. Ibid., min. 55, Ashton Warner to P.C.E.P., Jinja, 3.20.26. Kasimu Muwanika, a store-keeper with the Medical Department comp ined against the European Sanitation Officer for physical assault and against the Asian Clerk for racial insults and general victimization. Ibid., min. 102, Kasimu Muwanika to D.M.S.S., cc. C.S., 6.2.28. Results of these, however, do not appear in the file.

District Commissioners' offices for days or weeks.[1] After pursuing the brilliantly laid out case of Maikairi Ntwanga, the Secretariat was left in no doubt that Fyffe had transgressed the bounds of all normal practices in dealing with the native staff. Since this could not be admitted to the natives, the best that the Government could do to rectify the situation was to make Ntwanga's <u>Discharge Certificate</u> less injurious to himself, although Fyffe was unhappy about even this concession.[2] Ntwanga could not be reinstated in his post as this would be synonymous with confessing to Fyffe's high-handedness.

Clearly, after 1925 more and more Africans in government service were increasingly overcoming the docility generally expected of all "natives" in the dependencies. They no longer always turned the other cheek or remained tongue-tied in the face of obvious injustice at the hands of superior officers. The African protest movement and awakening can be said to have been quite firmly established by the mid-1920s among the educated classes in government employment. The BGNEA, however, was almost unknown to the public at large. The reason appears to be that it neither wanted to nor would have been permitted to conduct its campaign to ameliorate the conditions of service of its members through the press.[3] The power to remedy the various grievances brought to light by the BGNEA lay with the Government and not with the public. Thus, the BGNEA confined its appeals to the Government and was little known to the others until the late 1930s.

---

[1] U.N.A.S.M.P. 5533, min. 66, A.R. Lule, Secretary, BGNEA, to C.S., 3.18.27 and minutes 67 to 76, which contain the correspondence between the BGNEA and the Secretariat, the inter-Secretariat consultations and the correspondence between the Secretariat and Fyffe.

[2] Ibid., min. 76, Fyffe to C.S., 6.21.27. He felt that such an amendment was "tantamount to admitting that this man was entitled to quarters, which is not the case."

[3] Interviews: Kavuma, Kagobya, Mulira, Tomblings, J.E. de Souza and K.D. Gupta, 1970. All government servants were prohibited from communicating official matters or matters pertaining to their employment to the press. Also, in the case of the Africans, "public opinion" was hardly sympathetic.

From the NCS to the African Civil Service (ACS)

The presence of only five Africans in the NCS by early 1928 did disturb some government officials. The then Acting Chief Secretary, B.A. Warner, believed that he had unearthed a major obstacle hindering the progress of the NCS. This was the fact that the NCS and the Native Administrations were not interchangeable institutions with regard to pensions and gratuities. Warner's suggestion about making the two services interchangeable was accepted and the African staff could henceforward be guaranteed their compensation if they left the NCS for the much more attractive chieftaincies in the native governments. This measure was quickly passed as Whitehall, for no clear reason, had decided to relinquish its control over the conditions of service for the subordinate non-European staff to Entebbe.[1]

It so happened that by March 1928, the NCSB also felt the need to review the NCS salaries. Not only did it recommend increased pay for Makererians but also accepted the principle of annual automatic salary increments for them, subject to the normal fidelity and diligence certificates. This has been forced upon the Government by an insufficient enrollment, at Makerere, for the Medical, Veterinary, Agricultural and Surveying classes. Besides seriously impeding the prospects of Africanizing some of the existing subordinate services, a shortage of trained African personnel could endanger the plans to expand the scientific departments. Thus, once again, the Government decided to link the Makerere courses with government employment and to make the latter more attractive, thereby hoping to increase the enrollment for the professional courses at Makerere. The NCSB felt that the salary scales provided in the 1924 Regulations were "too vague and unattractive to furnish this inducement." The revised salaries advocated by the NCSB would, in fact, divide the NCS into two categories:

---

[1] U.N.A.S.M.P. A.2, min. 2, Ag. C.S. to C.S., 2.8.28; min. 24, S. of S. to Gowers, 10.16.28.

those with the professional Makerere qualifications, to whom the new terms would apply; and those without such qualifications who would continue under the old salary scales embodied in the <u>1924 Regulations</u>.[1]

Furthermore, Makererians with three to five years of training would be allowed to draw higher salaries than the existing maximum, shillings 240 (shs. 240/-) per month, that had been fixed for the Native Civil Servants. These significant concessions were made to this new class of professional Africans who were required to assist in extending the services of the scientific departments. Hitherto, the practice had been to fill junior grades with recruits from Britain or the Empire, particularly India, and later hope to localize some of those posts. The new approach in the scientific departments was to train the natives for the subordinate service at the outset and expand the services accordingly. Clerks, however, would not be permitted to exceed the maximum barrier of shs. 240/- p.m. This discrimination against them might have been influenced by the availability of Asian clerks in Uganda and East Africa generally. Also, the Makerere clerical course had yet to start and there may have been some reluctance to grant concessions which might later have to be withdrawn.

Entrance examinations for the NCS were not yet made competitive as the demand for educated Africans was then "certain to exceed the supply." However, competitive exams would become "advisable and necessary" in the future.

The Director of Education and the Secretary to the NCSB undertook to centralize the process of assessing the demand for Makerere trained clerks and professionals and their distribution, each year, to the relevant departments. This was an additional

---

[1] U.N.A.S.M.P. 8819, min. 33, Gowers to S. of S., Confidential, 5.30.28; C.O. 536/148/20016; Gowers to S. of S., Confidential, 5.30.28 and enclosures 1 and 2 thereto. See also J.E. Goldthorpe, <u>An African Elite</u>, O.U.P., Nairobi, 1965, pp. 9-10, 88. It is to the products of these courses at Makerere that the term "professionals" was applied and is used to refer to them, in this study.

measure to ensure that the NCS did make some progress, this time. If this new system succeeded, the Government hoped that all future recruitment of qualified African staff would be controlled by the NCSB and individual government officials would no longer be left to their own devices to fill the vacancies in their departments. Any natives educated abroad could join the NCS if they held recognized qualifications or passed an entrance examination.

On the whole, the new proposals of the NCSB were an aberration from the previous uncompromising stand taken by the Government against its African staff. They had to be introduced quickly, as the NCSB put it, "if the best material was to be obtained for clerical and professional posts."[1]

The Colonial Office promptly approved the recommended changes.[2] As the Treasury had, for no single definable reason, now surrendered its control over Uganda's finances,[3] the Colonial Office decided to leave the man-on-the-spot to resolve most local issues within the bounds of general policy laid down from London.[4]

These modifications in the 1924 Regulations did succeed in bringing about a slight improvement in the situation. More Africans in government employment sought membership in the NCS and by mid-1929 the NCSB had admitted ten of them.[5] Many pending applications to join the NCS had not been processed as the NCSB had decided to drastically overhaul that service. The three major changes recommended by the NCSB involved the institution of an exclusive African Civil Service (ACS), the substitution of the 1924 Regulations with the 1929 Regulations which would govern the ACS,

---

[1] C.O. 536/148/20016, enc. 1 in Gowers to S. of S., Confidential, 5.30.28.

[2] U.N.A.S.M.P. 8819, min. 39, Telegram, S. of S. to Governor, 7.17.28.

[3] C.O. 536/148/20016, minute by Eastwood, 7.11.28: "As Uganda is no longer under Treasury control, the details of the scheme may now? be left to the Governor." However, no clue is provided to the relaxation of the Treasury's control.

[4] Ibid., minute by Steel, 7.16.28.

[5] The Uganda Gazette, 10.15.27 to 7.31.29.

and the conversion of the executive NCSB into an advisory African Civil Service Board (ACSB). The main idea behind these improvisations--in the evidently unmanageable problem of devising a mutually acceptable formula for the contented employment of skilled Africans in the Protectorate Government--was to reduce the pension commitments of the Government and to simultaneously raise the status of the professionally trained Africans in government service.

This new scheme was to be executed at the expense of non-professional and non-clerical African staff. Artisans and allied categories would be barred from the pensionable establishment in the interest of economy. Since 1928, the NCSB had increasingly felt that the 1924 Regulations, which entitled many categories of African employees to attain pensionable status, had become obsolete in this respect. It was argued that the pensionable establishment should be restricted to the "New African" with better education only.

However, the door of the professionalized ACS would be kept open to those Africans already in the Government, with long service and experience but without the necessary paper qualifications--if they could pass the equivalent of Makerere examinations. Since the vast majority of the African employees would be excluded from the ACS, the NCSB proposed to compensate them with a higher gratuity scale. This would entail some amendments to the 1925 Regulations. In other words, all those Africans who could not enter the ACS would automatically be covered by the amended 1925 Regulations, which were to be renamed the ACS Regulations, Part II.[1]

To boost the recruitment for the ACS, the Government would inform students intending to attend Makerere, that they stood an excellent chance of joining the ACS. This measure would not pose any extra financial burden as such recruits would "in most cases replace Asiatic, or even European personnel, who would be employed on a pensionable basis." Similarly, school-leavers would be briefed, before they went to Makerere, if there were likely to be

---

[1] C.O. 536/156/20396, no. 247, Gowers to S. of S., 6.17.29; U.N.A.S.M.P. 8819, min. 45, excerpts from NCSB minutes, 11.9.28.

no more vacant posts for them in the ACS. If such a situation arose, the Government would later decide whether or not to confer all the other privileges of the ACS minus the pension rights on candidates with a Makerere education who could not be absorbed by its pensionable establishment.

The decision to transform the NCSB--which was to be renamed the ACSB--from an executive to an advisory body was influenced by the desire to bring it on a par with the Asian CSB. Henceforth, the last word on all matters pertaining to the ACS would be that of the Governor as the new executive body. This arrangement also obviated the possibility of any resentment among those Heads of Departments who would not sit on the ACSB and yet would have to accept its directives regarding the control of the native staff in their departments.

The Government further substituted the adjective African for Native in the revised regulations, so as to bring it in conformity with the adjectives European and Asian applied to the other two branches of the Civil Service in Uganda. This terminological alteration was additionally desirable "because the Government's Swahili programme" would "necessitate the employment for considerable time of a number of Swahilis by the Protectorate Government." Finally, the Government envisaged--as a result of the expanding communications with countries adjacent to Uganda--the employment of suitably qualified natives from the neighboring territories.[1]

With these changes, the racially differentiated branches of the Uganda Civil Service (UCS) were formally endorsed. Although the 1929 Regulations were quite meticulously prepared,[2] they gave scant consideration to the wishes of the BGNEA previously expressed in its several petitions. African civil servants were denied free housing and would be required to pay a rent if allotted government quarters. However, those African civil servants, the nature of whose work made it incumbent upon them to be constantly available

---

[1] Ibid.

[2] Ibid., enc. in no. 247; Regulations for the African Civil Service, Part I, Govt. Press: Hereinafter the 1929 Regulations.

for duty in hospitals, schools or "other such institutions," would be exempted from rents.

The improved salary scales introduced in 1928, which were related to the length of training at Makerere, were retained.[1] A "Special Grade" (£100 by £10 to £200 p.a.) was created for Africans with not less than years' service who held "positions of exceptional trust and responsibility." If favorably recommended by their Heads of Departments, such Africans could attain to the Special Grade.

The fine of ten shillings--which the BGNEA had rejected as "excessive" in 1925--for each offense of misconduct, disrespect, disobedience, unpunctuality and carelessness or negligence in the performance of duties, was retained. In fact, the Heads of Departments were empowered to delegate all the disciplinary powers to any other officers in their departments "to inflict fines up to the above maximum, with such limitations and conditions" as they might think fit. This second part of this regulation was ill-advised since it could afford non-African superior officers the opportunity to harass African civil servants if the former thought that the latter were likely to encroach upon their preserves. The already strained race relations in the Civil Service could, and indeed did, become more embittered because of such practices. (Motani, 1975)

The award of pensions, gratuities and other allowances was made conditional upon rendering loyal and diligent service. A minimum of 15 years with the Government would be necessary to

---

[1] Grades A and B would apply to the Clerks; Grade C to the Native School Masters; Grade D to the Departmental Assistants and Grade E to those medical students who successfully completed the five years' course at Makerere and Mulago Hospital. Their starting salaries were to be based on the length of their courses. Students with three years of training would commence work at a salary of 95/- per month, rising annually by 8/- p.m.; those with four years of training would receive 110- p.m., rising annually by 9/- p.m., and finally those who had five years of training would start at 140/- p.m. with annual increments of 10/- p.m.

The proposed one year's clerical course at Makerere was extended to two years and the students completing it would be paid 80/- p.m. with annual increments of 6/- p.m. Hitherto, youths aged between 16 and 18 years, with no knowledge of office work, had been directly recruited from the mission-schools to fill the junior clerical vacancies. They were paid from 40/- p.m. to 60/-p.m. and were hardly thought to be an asset to the offices.

qualify for pensions or gratuities which would be granted on completion of 30 years of pensionable service or on attaining the age of 55. Furthermore, the Protectorate and the Native Governments were recognized as interchangeable with regard to superannuation.

When the service of an African civil servant seconded to a native administration was either completed or terminated, the Governor, at his discretion, could readmit him to the ACS. African civil servants so transfered to the native governments would qualify for gratuities if they had completed at least five years' service with the Protectorate Government. To be eligible for pensions, however, "not less than 15 years' aggregate service with the Protectorate Government" was prescribed.[1]

To sum up the significance of the 1929 Regulations, they proposed to convert the NCS into a restricted establishment for the new African elite. Recruits for it would be drawn primarily from Makerere--East Africa's highest educational center which had emerged and had been moulded in response to the ever-increasing manpower needs of the various government departments.

The Colonial Office recognized this at once. Eastwood commented: "The Permanent Civil Service will be very aristocratic and exclusive..." He was quite astonished to learn that so far only ten Africans had been admitted to the NCS. On the whole, he recommended that approval could be given to Uganda Authorities without any consultations with the Secretary of State.[2] A.C.C. Parkinson found nothing objectionable in the new proposals and endorsed Eastwood's views.[3] The Governor's covering dispatch as well as the 1929 Regulations had made both the rationale and the implications of the ACS very unequivocal. Acheson wrote:

> I do not see how we can criticise any of these proposals. They represent, of course, a pretty complete reversal of the policy adopted only 7 years ago, and a change

---

[1] The 1929 Regs., para. 13-13(8).

[2] C.O. 536/156/20396, minute by Eastwood, 7.29.29 on no. 247, Gowers to S. of S., 6.17.29.

[3] Ibid., minute by Parkinson, 8.24.29.

from a special system devised to meet a special situation to more orthodox methods; but the local government alone is in a position to judge whether conditions justify the change. If they are satisfied, the Secretary of State will not wish to object.[1]

The Treasury, as has been noted earlier, no longer exercised tight control over the colonial budgets. Even if it had, the ACS was very much along the conventional lines which the London officials could comprehend. There were, this time, no artisans or headmen to be included in the ACS. Acheson observed with satisfaction that the exclusion of the artisans from the ACS would be "without untoward results," and that as more Africans with better education became available, the Uganda Government would introduce competitive exams for the ACS.[2]

As regards the 1929 Regulations Part II, namely the revised non-pensionable 1925 Regulations, the Colonial Office approved the arrangement advocated by the Uganda Authorities for some natives not in the ACS. If an African employee became--as a result of his service with the Government--completely divorced from his tribal environment and found it impossible to revert to tribal life, upon retirement he was to be granted a pension instead of a gratuity, or alternatively a substantially increased gratuity. This was a benevolent, protective device for those African employees who were liable to be detribalized through prolonged exposure to urban and western ways of life.

The approval of the 1929 Regulations emphasized the racially differentiated branches of the UCS, with pay and privileges generally distributed, in descending order, to Europeans, Asians and Africans. However, the ACS with its exclusive complexion became more dignified and elevated than its predecessor. Some

---

[1] Ibid., memorandum on no. 247 by Acheson, 8.23.29. Generally, it seems decisions on all but the most vital matters were taken by the top C.O. officials without even the knowledge of the S. of S. Everything was done by the highest officials in the name of S. of S.

[2] Ibid.

notable concessions contained in the 1929 Regulations entitled the African civil servants, just as much as European and Asian civil servants. to annual salary increments "subject to the usual diligence and fidelity certificate."[1] The "Special Grade" constituted a kind of a safety-valve in the ACS to permit exceptionally meritorious Africans to cross the racial barrier and draw salaries far above those generally prescribed for that particular ethnic group.

The official outlook on the whole subject was now much more charitable than it had been during 1925-28. The Acting Chief Secretary, E. L. Scott, circularized the Heads of Departments to implement the 1929 Regulations in a sympathetic vein. He reminded the Heads of Departments that the Service Books--with their pejorative connotations--which had been a part of the NCS were abolished and that the records of African Civil Servants "will be kept in the same manner as are those of European or Asiatic Civil Servants."[2] Thus, paradoxically, the 1929 Regulations underlined the fairly rigid distinctions among the three branches of the UCS, and, at the same time, they removed many discriminating features of the NCS, bringing the ACS closer to the European and the Asian Civil Services.

The ACS Establishment consisted of 150 clerical and 100 professional posts. All admissions would be made only to fill the vacancies in the establishment which was to vary from time to time. At the inception of the ACS 19 posts, 12 clerical and seven professional, had been filled.[3] Some of these candidates were presumably salvaged from the wreckage of the NCS and others probably entered it from Makerere or after passing an equivalent examination.

---

[1] Makerere Library, G. EAU. 902, Uganda Non-Serial: Circular no. 17 of 1930.

[2] Ibid., C.S.'s office to all Heads of Depts., 10.30.30. Non-African staff's records were kept in individual files.

[3] Ibid.

Changing Fortunes of the ACS

The inauguration of the 1929 Regulations seemed to herald a new era of an elitist ACS which would compare favorably with its European and Asian counterparts and eventually help to Africanize some sections of the UCS. However, this was not to be quite the case. One of the drawbacks was an inherently debilitating factor in the ACS, namely the provision for transfering African civil servants to the Native Governments.

In the age of Indirect Rule and trusteeship, the colonial administrators were torn between the localization of the central government and the modernization of the native authorities. The general British mood and the particular African partiality for service with their own tribal organizations spelled the diversion of educated Africans from the Protectorate to the Native Governments, thus depriving the ACS of its pride and some of its best minds. However, this system satisfied Entebbe, the African elite and Whitehall.[1] The Protectorate Government tended to regard the employment of Africans in its departments as a rewarding exercise in preparing them for service with their tribal authorities. The Governor explained that the majority of the youths entering the ACS would "be of a class" from which chieftaincies in the tribal administrations could be filled:

> ... The Board [NCSB] consider it of the greatest importance that these young men should be encouraged to take the Makerere course and to serve at least five years with a department of the Protectorate Government before entering the service of a Native Government. The personal training and the experience of Government methods and standards thus gained will, it is represented, be of the greatest benefit to the men themselves, to the Native Government with which they subsequently serve, and to the Protectorate generally.[2]

---

[1] See "Future Policy in regard to Eastern Africa," Cmd. 2904, H.M.S.O., 1927, p. 5; "Memorandum on Native Policy in East Africa," Cmd. 3573, H.M.S.O., 1930, p. 7.

[2] C.O. 536/156/20396, no. 247.

It would appear that education at school, by itself, was not deemed sufficient for inculcating western standards of efficiency, punctuality, probity and the like into the future native public servants who were expected to enrich their own local governments and bring them in close proximity to the central bureaucracy. Before the arrival of the missionaries and the establishment of colonial rule, the Kabaka's court and the chiefs' enclosures had been the traditional avenues through which social distinction was attained. During the first two decades of the twentieth century, the mission high schools which taught English replaced the traditional kigalagalas in leadership training. By the 1920s, service with the Protectorate Government represented yet another stage, perhaps the most critical one, in the making of the future chiefs. This system of appointing chiefs was detrimental to the ACS as the transfer of native personnel was almost inevitably from the Protectorate to the Native Governments and rarely vice versa. (Mulira, 1950; Fallers, 1964)

African Opposition to the Dilution of the ACS

Not surprisingly, the Asian and European immigrant interest groups were somewhat apprehensive of the ACS's potential overall effects. Since the Asian clerks would be most directly affected by the Africanization policy, the Asian community requested the Government to clarify its policy. The Government confirmed that its official policy was to encourage Africans to replace Asian clerks but no Asian civil servants with even an implied promise of permanent employment would be affected.[1]

Unlike the Asians, the small unofficial European community in Uganda had no direct interest in civil service appointments. Its representatives in the Legco were mainly concerned with efficient and economical working of the bureaucracy. European leaders were highly critical of academic education for the Africans and the

---

[1] Legislative Council (Legco) summary, 11.27.30, pp. 6-7.

"very generous rates of pay" proposed for Makererians joining the ACS.[1]

However, it was the actual official European ambivalence, occasionally bordering on subversion, coupled with the global slump of the 1930s, that ultimately injured the growth of the ACS. On the one hand, Heads of Departments were directed to be very strict with those African Civil Servants who were still on probation. Only those probationers who convincingly showed signs of acquiring "an intimate knowledge of their work and an efficiency in performing it sufficient to justify their retention," should be allowed to remain in employment. Though these might have been standard instructions regarding other probationers, in the case of the African civil servants they could easily be exploited by officials eager to retain their experienced Asian staff on grounds that Africans could not take over without a decline in the efficiency of the Civil Service.

On the other hand, the departmental heads were reminded that African probationers should receive every opportunity to prove themselves. Moreover, their supervision was to be undertaken only by those senior officials who were in charge of government offices and departments. This was presumably aimed at discouraging the unwise practice, among some European officials, of delegating the supervision of Africans to the Asian staff. However, there were no provisions to ascertain that this particular piece of advice would be followed--hence it continued to be ignored. D. G. Tomblings, Makerere's Principal, reporting on the 22 pioneer clerks who had just completed three years as probationers, disclosed that 16 of them had been confirmed in their appointments to the ACS; five were put on further probation

---

[1] The Uganda Herald, 12.5.30, pp. 21-22; Ibid., 1.30.31, p. 8. The total population of Uganda, in 1931, was 3.5 millions, 2,001 being Europeans and 14,150 being Asians. No separate figures for Goans or unofficial Europeans are available. Both Hindu and Muslim Asians were represented in the UCS but the Africans did not differentiate between them along religious lines. But Roman Catholic Goans tended to be seen apart from the rest of the Asians.

for one year and one of them was dismissed. He suspected that
where sympathetic supervision had been provided, the reports on
the clerks had been promising and vice versa. More ruefully, he
noted that some European officers had ignored official instructions and delegated supervision of probationers to Asian staff.[1]
If the British had been sincere in Africanizing the subordinate
clerical service in Uganda, this method of achieving it was patently obstructive to this desire.

However, it is significant that the few pioneer African
civil servants whose recollections could be recorded for this
study appear to have been more incensed by British than by Asian
behavior in this matter. They were conscious that the British
officials held the balance and could, if they genuinely wished,
turn the scales in the Africans' favor. They complained that,
until the 1930s, African civil servants rarely had direct access
to European officials.[2] They found little sense in lodging
complaints against Asian civil servants through the Asian intermediaries who first dealt with all African grievances.

The Asians, quite understandably, were given to preserving
the status quo. They must have succumbed to the natural and human
instinct for survival, thus keeping the Africans out of a host of
subordinate and middle grade positions. However, it has been
contended by several Asian civil servants that even if they had
had the willingness to share their knowledge and experience of
office work with their competitors, they seldom found time to
do this. All the drudgery and many of the normal duties of the
office superintendents and other European officers were reported
to have been frequently loaded upon the Asian clerks. Recriminations aside, the strongest Asian argument remained that the supervision of the African clerks was officially assigned to the

---

[1] Ibid., 12.20.33; UNASMP A. 28/B, min. 35, 12.31.31.

[2] Interviews: Paulo Kavuma, A. L. Kagobya, David Senfuma, Y. K. Lubogo, S. B. K. Musoke and Paulo Semakula, 1970.

office superintendents who all happened to be Europeans.[1]

In view of the avowed government policy of replacing Asian clerks with Africans, this European behavior is somewhat bewildering and the reasons for it are largely speculative. Contact with the Goans in India and later in East Africa had generated "Goanophilia," among the British administrators as a whole, marked by excessive fondness of and dependence on the Goan clerks. Africans, too, though critical of the Goans for blocking their progress, were envious of their clerical skill and uprightness.[2]

Connected with the anxiety about a decline in the standards of the clerical service through Africanization, there may have been dormant fears among the junior European office staff that the dilution of the Asian cadre would soon make them vulnerable too. The retention of Asian clerks, besides guaranteeing continued high standards, would offer such Europeans some protection as a result of the buffer-zones formed by the Asians. It is in this context that the relative fervor of the Secretariat and other senior well-entrenched officials and the inhibitions of the lesser European civil servants about Africanization make sense. However, in most African eyes the obvious culprits cramping their progress appeared to be the Asians whose predominance in the subordinate service could not escape notice.

Unfortunately for the ACS, its development coincided with the depression which affected Uganda critically after 1930. Consequently, immigrant assaults upon it continued and even some top-ranking officials turned against it for economic and selfish reasons. Uganda was not as badly hit by the slump as it might have been, owing to a fairly large surplus balance amassed under Gowers.[3] However, as he wanted to conserve the surplus balance

---

[1] Interviews: James E. de Souza, August 1970; K. D. Gupta and Haribhai Patel of the Asiatic CSA; discussions with several Entebbe Goan civil servants, April-June 1970.

[2] See reference 2, p.

[3] Gowers wanted to maintain the surplus balance over £1 million. See K. Ingham, *The Making of Modern Uganda*, London, 1958, pp. 204-205.

for gloomier years, curbing governmental expenditure now became an administrative imperative.

It is interesting to note that both the Finance Committee, appointed in 1931, and the Executive Council opposed an immediate introduction of income tax or levy on official salaries as unnecessary and untimely.[1] European pay and terms of service could not be adjusted unilaterally by the Protectorate Government since they had to be coordinated with the Colonial Service elsewhere. The relatively under-privileged Asian staff aroused little public or official criticism at this time. Thus attention shifted to the ACS. Besides being the weakest branch of the UCS, its terms of service could be determined locally although Whitehall's approval would be necessary.[2]

Diminishing confidence in Makerere clerks and the slump prompted the Government to amend the 1929 Regulations whereby the individual and not the post in the ACS carried pensionable status. Hitherto, of the 150 clerical and 100 professional posts in the ACS, 54 clerical and 31 professional vacancies had been filled.[3] The task of devising a new salary scale for the African staff was entrusted, in June 1933, to the African Subordinate Establishments Committee (A.S.E.C.). It was composed of senior European officials who invited departmental heads to offer their views on the subject. Most of them felt that all the privileges conferred upon the clerks by the 1929 Regulations were not really necessary and that the salary scales had been too liberally conceived.[4]

The ASEC recognized that the Africanization of the clerical service had made little headway. European departmental chiefs were

---

[1] Report of the Finance Committee, Entebbe, 1931, para 14(5): Exco. minutes, 8.27.32.

[2] Legco summary, 7.31.33, p. 56.

[3] C.O. 536/177/3571, Governor to S. of S., 4.7.33.

[4] C.O. 536/185/40035, Report of the ASEC, April 1934, enc. in no. 40, Governor to S. of S., 2.5.35; U.N.A.S.M.P. A.28/4, passim.

rebuked for their reluctance to give the Africans a fair chance; closer, more sympathetic supervision was urged. The Africans' "natural lack of self-assertiveness" was also singled out as an important factor.[1] However, the ASEC's recommendations actually amounted to stripping the African clerks of their most cherished privileges. The 1929 Regulations were upheld for the professional African civil servants, but clerks were to be placed together with the rest of the non-pensionable staff under the 1925 Regulations. The payment of an acting allowance to the African staff, when performing the duties of higher grade officers, was also challenged. The ASEC contended that the opportunity of gaining experience while acting in a higher post was in itself a fair reward. The Africans had put up a vigorous fight for pensions during the 1920s. The ASEC now wanted the African clerks to forfeit not only their pension rights and subscribe to a provident fund but also to accept inferior salaries. The new grading system aimed at rewarding the meritorious by accelerated promotions and holding back the mediocrities. Though this was a fair proposition, the starting pay of all the employees was so drastically reduced that it was certain to arouse much ill-feeling among all Africans concerned.

The new scale contained six grades. The ASEC had already recommended that clerical training at Makerere should cease and that learners should be recruited directly from the schools. These learners would enter Grade VI at shs. 20/- p.m. for two years. They would then spend six years in each of the five superior grades before reaching the top of Grade I, which stopped at shs. 200/- p.m.[2]

These recommendations were patently retrograde for the African clerks. Admission to the ACS was to be suspended, salaries would be cut, the gap between the African and Asian clerical services would widen and the African clerks would generally be degraded. The Africans were staggered by the ASEC's proposals which were

---

[1] Report of the ASEC, para. 5-6.

[2] Ibid., para. 7-23.

interpreted as a gross and studied insult. The BGNEA, which had changed its name to the British Government African Employees Association (B.G.A.E.A.)--probably as a belated reaction to the pejorative connotation of the word "native" or as a result of the replacement of the NCS by the ACS--petitioned the Governor to delay implementing the new scheme until the Africans had had the opportunity to speak their minds.

The Africans were amazed that a general reduction in their salaries was being contemplated when their standard of living was rising. Clerks could hardly maintain the standard of dressing and cleanliness expected of them on the current salaries. It was further represented that the new grades for learner-clerks would jeopardize their marriage prospects. Custom required Africans to marry between the age of 20 and 30 but the proposed salary of shs. 20/- p.m. would make this totally impossible for the junior clerks.[1] The BGAEA appealed that the Africans, who were subjected to disproportionate direct and indirect taxation compared to the other communities, should be granted "a reasonably good pay, so as to ensure civilized and clean habits of life" among them. (Ingham, 1958; Apter, 1967)

This last point about good living was particularly valid as the Government had recently staged a Public Health Exhibition in order to encourage better homes, good health and a balanced diet among the people.[2] The BGAEA, hence, aptly remarked that what the Government preached to the Africans was unlikely to be practiced by its own employees if their small salaries were to suffer further mutilations. The years to come looked even more somber: "The idea of saving up something for a 'rainy day' for the education of our children is out of the question."

Although the ASEC had not discussed the African housing problem, the BGAEA exploited the occasion to the hilt and recapitulated forcefully its manifold grievances. If they wished to live

---

[1] C.O. 536/185/40035, BGAEA to Governor, 8.22.34.

[2] Uganda Annual Report (U.A.R.), 1934, pp. 16-17.

near their places of work, the Africans had to build their own homes on government land. Not only did the Government charge them a rent for "the temporary occupation of Crown Land" but also refused compensation to the owners of such houses when they were transferred to other stations. For the umpteenth time, the Africans pleaded with the Government that the introduction of housing allowances or free government quarters would assuage this hardship. This was stated to be a crucial question because in some instances where African clerks had taken over from the Asians, they had found it very difficult to maintain the same punctuality since they lived far away from the offices.

The Africans also disapproved of the government vans--which were provided when the African staff went on leave--on the grounds that they were suitable only for transporting goods. Besides being slow, they were not weatherproof and did not convey the passengers beyond the nearest government post in the district where leave was to be spent. The Africans wished to arrange their own transport and be paid for this by the Government.[1]

Both the ACSB and Governor Bourdillon (1932-1935) had basically accepted the report of the ASEC. However, Bourdillon was somewhat sceptical about the success of the new scheme which he thought was rather severe upon the clerks. He cautioned that "it might be found necessary to revert in course of time to conditions more attractive than those recommended by the Committee if an African Clerical Service is to be built up to the standard of efficiency and loyalty attained by the Asiatic Clerical Service which it is designed to replace." Clearly sympathetic to the African staff, he forwarded the petition from the BGAEA to London so that the Colonial Office might obtain a deeper understanding of the African grievances. However, Bourdillon gave his consent to the recommendations of the ASEC in the hope that some useful experience might be gained in devising a mutually agreeable solution to the question of African employment.[2]

---

[1] C.O. 536/185/40035, BGAEA to Governor, 8.22.34.

[2] Ibid. no. 40, Gov. to S. of S., 2.5.35.

The Governor's observations and the BGAEA's enlightening petition evoked a genial exposition of the intricacies which retarded the advancement of the East African natives as a whole:

> The general attitude of the people in Uganda towards their natives <u>appears</u> to be that of the wonder and doubt with which one looks upon the doings of a performing sealion. They seem astonished to find that the African can do anything at all and still more astonished to find that he can do some things well and that he holds out a definite promise of a still better achievement.... People in Uganda have probably been hypnotised by the excellence of their Asiatic clerks and have, in the past, taken the view that since equally good material was not forthcoming immediately from the African, it was no good trying the African. This attitude of mind is, I think, unfair to the native population.[1]

Although it cannot be determined how others in the Colonial Office saw the situation, Flood's own apprehension about African prospects in the Uganda Administration was astute. He felt that the Uganda Government should be informed plainly that it should be satisfied with the African clerks and make the maximum use of them in the Civil Service. Flood was taken aback by the dismal salary of shs. 20/- planned for the clerks and was totally dismayed by the projected contributory pension scheme:

> There is a tendency in East Africa and especially in Uganda, to throw aside native and Asiatic employees when they cease to be useful and to contend that they ought not on any account be made pensionable, hence a lot of talk about provident funds and contributory pensions.

If the "unfortunate employee" was to be forced to contribute to a fund, Flood stressed that he should then be paid a much bigger salary. He rejected the idea that Africans should be discharged from the Government because of inefficiency. Once a person had been recruited into the Civil Service, he should be given every opportunity to prove himself in other departments if he was unfit in his initial appointment, but never dismissed from the service.[2]

---

[1] Ibid., minute by J.E.W. Flood, 4.29.35, on no. 40 and enclosures thereto.

[2] Ibid.

However, Flood's vehement sentiments were not made known to the Uganda Government in their entirety. The Secretary of State approved the recommendations of the ASEC purely as an interim measure, with some reservations about the very low pay for the clerks. The Colonial Office regarded free pensions as more appropriate for the African clerical staff. However, should the Uganda Government choose to remain adamant on this point, it was advised to raise the African salaries to a level "sufficient to enable them to make the suggested annual contributions without undue hardship." That the Colonial Office tried to acquaint the Uganda Authorities with the difficulties besetting its African servants testified to the ability of the BGAEA to conduct its affairs quite effectively. Indeed, some parts of the dispatch from London read as if they had been written by the BGAEA:

> A Government clerk is, during his working life, cut off from the normal life of his tribe and it seems possible that the tendency will be that he will not be re-absorbed into tribal life on his retirement in the same way that an old labourer will be.

London was concerned that the African clerks should be able to continue living in the same manner after retirement as during their service with the Government and free pensions were deemed essential for this purpose. Nevertheless, despite London's awareness of the adverse effects of the Asian factor on Africanization, and in the light of its concern about the racialistic undertones of the new Uganda scheme, it is rather strange that Whitehall did not press for the replacement of the Asian clerks. Only a very faint reminder about adhering to the ultimate goal of Africanizing the clerical service was sent.[1]

At the end of 1934, the UCS comprised 530 European officials, 300 Asians--mainly engaged in clerical duties, and 130 pensionable Africans. The foundations of the ACS had already been laid and the Ugandan Africans were said to be adopting service with the Protectorate Government "as a career." (Thomas & Scott, 1935)

---

[1] Ibid., S. of S to Governor (Draft), 5.4.35.

While this was true of the professional and technical staff, it was not quite so with the clerks who controlled the BGAEA.

The BGAEA was very much in the dark about the fate of its petition of August 22, 1934. After two further reminders in October of the same year and in February of the following year, a reply was elicited from the Secretariat.[1] Thus, it was in March 1935 that the Africans officially learned that the 1929 Regulations, amended in accordance with the ASEC's report, had been presented to the Colonial Office for approval. While London's sanction was being awaited, the Chief Secretary briefed the Africans about the changes that would almost certainly come into effect. They were told about the definite restriction of the ACS to the professional civil servants and the probable introduction of a provident fund.

The Chief Secretary brushed aside most of the African demands as he found them unreasonable. Neither did he wish to debate the subject with the BGAEA since the ACSB was still looking into the matter. However, he did elaborate on the new grading system for the benefit of the restive clerks. Grade VII would embrace all beginners in the technical and specialist trades. Their salaries would not exceed shs. 30/- p.m. On the completion of their training, apprentices would be appointed to either Grade VI or Grade V according to ability but their maximum salary would be shs. 45/- p.m. The main interest of the BGAEA, however, was centered on the grades affecting the clerks. Unfortunately for them, the new provisions were heavily biased against them.

Those African students who desired to become clerks would have to enter Grade VI on two years' probation at a salary of shs. 20/- p.m. The Government would allow successful candidates to proceed to Grade V and dispense with the services of the unsuccessful ones. Salary increments, within each grade from Grade V to I would be dependent on diligence and efficiency certificates. But the clerks, specifically, were promised every

---

[1] C.O. 536/185/40035, C.S. to Secretary, BGAEA, 3.16.35.

opportunity of learning the duties of the higher grade posts and of seeking transfers to other departments, if they wished, though their request for acting allowances was categorically refused.[1]

Theoretically, under the 1929 Regulations, African civil servants could gain promotions on passing an "efficiency bar" and if favorably recommended by their Heads of Departments.[2] Thus, deserving African civil servants could periodically expect to ascend the financial ladder. Now, by relating the promotion prospects for clerks from one grade to another with the actual vacancies in the departmental establishments, the clerks would be deprived of a supremely attractive inducement. By itself, this may have been a sensible economical measure but in this particular case it was a step causing much anguish to its victims.

The Chief Secretary's reply temporarily paralyzed the BGAEA, then led by Lwanga (Vice President), Simoni Mwanjuzi (Honorary Secretary) and Yokana Mukora (Honorary Treasurer).[3] Nearly two months elapsed before any reply at all was made. Nevertheless the BGAEA did score a modest success when it prevailed upon the Governor to telegraph the Colonial Office to either delay or reconsider its ruling on the ASEC's report since the Africans wished to submit another petition.[4] Bourdillon's decision to suspend action on the recommendations of the ASEC, until the Colonial Office had studied the new petition, was a mark of respect to the BGAEA, described by him as "a responsible body." Bourdillon's sympathy, as far as the salary scale was concerned, lay with the petitioners. However, he had supported the wishes of his

---

[1] Ibid.

[2] The 1929 Regulations, para. 4-5. For an explanation of "efficiency bar", see p. 61, below.

[3] C.O. 536/185/40035, BGAEA to S. of S., 5.29.35. No information was obtainable about these men except that Mwanjuzi was a clerk in the Secretariat. The post of President seems to have been unoccupied in 1935.

[4] Ibid. Confidential telegram, Governor to S. of S., 5.13.35.

senior officers in the ACSB and the ASEC because they were reputed to be intimately familiar with the African way of life. His approval was given "on the distinct understanding...that the situation will be watched and the question reconsidered should the proposals prove to be unsatisfactory in operation."

As far as the other repeated African assertions went, the Governor felt that it would be helpful to Entebbe if London showed its teeth to the Africans. He particularly advised that the demand for free quarters or allowances in lieu "must be firmly resisted." Government vehicles used for transporting the African staff to and from leave were admittedly uncomfortable. The Governor regretted that the Africans would have to endure this hardship since it was financially difficult to provide alternative facilities.

The reception that the Colonial Office would accord to the petition was, thus, already influenced by the Governor. Bourdillon further specified that: "The revised regulations in fact affect only the African Clerical Service, of which the petitioning Association is primarily representative."[1] The Governor had rightly sensed that only a minority, though an important one, of the African staff was involved and it had exaggerated both the grievances and the yearning for reforms.[2]

The Uganda Government justified the preferential treatment accorded to the non-Africans, above all, on the grounds that Europeans and Asians were "overseas civil servants" whereas the Africans belonged to a "home civil service."[3] Indeed, this distinction had molded the civil service structure in Uganda as elsewhere in East Africa and was frequently evoked to defend the wide gulf

---

[1] Ibid., Governor to S. of S., Confidential, 6.24.35. Some of the monthly wages in Uganda, in 1935, were: houseboys, 30/- to 80/-; cooks, 25/- to 100/-; shop-assistants, 20/- to 60/-; clerks, 25/- to 240/-. See U.A.R. 1935, p. 31.

[2] Musoke, Semakula and Kagobya revealed, in 1970, that the Association always made inflated demands hoping to receive only moderate concessions.

[3] C.O. 536/185/40035, Governor to S. of S., Confidential, 6.24.35.

separating the conditions of service for the Africans and the non-Africans.

As in previous petitions, a wide range of members' problems were recapitulated by the BGAEA in 1935. The African leaders were at considerable pains to convey the ripples of anger and discontent that the report of the ASEC had allegedly stirred up throughout the rank and file of the African personnel. It was emphasized that the petition--signed by the executive and the members of the BGAEA--had resulted from a mass meeting held on May 3, 1935. This was presumably mentioned so that the petition might not be taken purely as a document of ills peculiar to the clerks only.

Referring to the British attempts to stabilize African conditions of employment during 1913-1914 and the <u>1924</u> and <u>1925 Regulations</u>, the BGAEA now pointed out that the representatives of the African staff had not been consulted.[1] The implication seems to have been that this lack of direct consultations between the African staff and senior European officials, prior to the introduction of each new scheme for African civil servants, was a major cause of African discontent.

The ASEC had sought no evidence from BGAEA because the European members were believed to be adequately conversant with the real needs of the Africans.[2] Thus, as in the past, on this occasion, too, the Government did not quite have its fingers on the pulse of the African staff. The diagnosis, conducted from a distance without actually bothering to ask the patients to state their symptoms, were inevitably inaccurate and the remedies prescribed were correspondingly inept. The African clerks could not fathom the official attitude towards them. They found the Government either inaccessible to logic or deliberately inclined to degrading the African clerical establishment. The BGAEA contended that improved education was continuously stimulating the Africans

---

[1] Ibid., BGAEA to S. of S., 5.29.35.

[2] Ibid., Governor to S. of S., Confidential, 6.24.35. See on this Cyril Ehrlich, "Some Social and Economic Implications of Paternalism in Uganda," <u>J.A.H.</u>, iv, 2 (1963), pp. 275-285.

to raise their standard of living and that any changes in their conditions of service should foster, not cramp, this healthy aspiration.[1] The Governor, however, rejected the claim that the Africans were entitled to better financial rewards because many African clerks had a superior style of living compared to the Asian clerks.[2]

Once again, African resentment against British partiality towards the Asian staff was evident. The petitioners complained about this discrimination, questioned its validity and called for parity with the Asian personnel.[3]

The practice of calculating the true value of African labor on the assumption that all Africans grew their own food or lived with friends or relatives who owned shambas (vegetable and fruit gardens) greatly troubled the Africans. The BGAEA declared this to be largely no longer true and also protested that whether an African grew his own food or not should have no bearing on his salary.[4] A "Long-Scale" in a civil service ensures that advancement for the staff is subject to the passing of "efficiency bars" at fixed points in the scale, not to the occurrence of vacancies. "By this means, blocks in promotion would be avoided and every officer could look forward with certainty to the prospect of reaching the maximum, provided that he maintained his efficiency." (Jeffries, 1938) Such a long-scale had been incorporated into the 1929 Regulations for the clerical and professional African civil servants. Understandably, the clerks were alarmed when they realized that the long-scale would disappear, condemning many of them "to remain on fixed, non-incremental scales through no fault of theirs, if no vacancies existed in the higher grades."

---

[1] Ibid., BGAEA to S. of S., 5.29.35.

[2] Ibid., Gov. to S. of S., Confidential, 6.24.35.

[3] Ibid., BGAEA to S. of S., 5.29.35.

[4] Ibid.

The BGAEA warned the Government that the adoption of the revised salary scales and other retrogressive measures would discourage many Africans from seeking higher education and only the worst element in the educated community would choose government service as a career. There was a clear indication in these outpourings that the Africans would only opt for service with the Protectorate Government in the last resort and even then it would be a transit stage to more attractive employment. The petition did not rule out mass resignations if the new salary scales did not permit the African civil servants "to live in a manner becoming their status." The Government, it seems, took this as a bluff rather than a real threat.

In conclusion the petitioners declared that they were utterly astounded and profoundly saddened by what appeared to be a double-faced Africanization policy of the Government. Though they were bitter about the large number of Asians in the Civil Service who created barriers in their paths, they were more offended by the failure of the Protectorate Government to act decisively in favor of the Africans:

> The Association respectfully submits that its members are entitled to receive from the Government at least as much consideration as is given to Government Asiatic Employees. The disparity in the emoluments of the Asiatic and African employees is disheartening to the latter.

It was painful for them to realize that the highest salaries they could ever expect were little different from the starting pay of most Asian employees. They could not reconcile all this "with the fact that an increasing number of natives have a higher standard of living than a large number of non-natives, and with Government's admission that the time is ripe for Africans to replace Asians in most clerical posts..." All government efforts to devise suitable regulations for the African staff would be futile unless the Africans were given a share in formulating them or until their views were sought at first hand and subsequently reflected in the regulations. They pressed for the immediate appointment of a special investigator to make fresh proposals about their conditions of employment, after seeking evidence from the African staff.[1]

The Colonial Office, forewarned by the Governor that the BGAEA, under the sway of the clerks, had somewhat overstated its members' tribulations, accordingly regarded the petition as an over-dramatized case.[2] To be forewarned is to be fore-prejudiced. On housing, A. D. Garson at the Colonial Office remarked that "...the Association are asking too much," and that a bad precedent would be created by granting free accommodation. As to traveling on lorries he felt "the Association are being hypersensitive."[3] However, S. Campbell of the East Africa Department commented:

> On studying the petition which is couched in very moderate and sensible language one cannot escape the impression that these people are just keeping their end up and that their grievances are not very dire.[4]

But J. E. W. Flood, previously sympathetic, was now unimpressed:

> The demands for free quarters, better travelling accommodations and more leave are rather absurd and they must know it.[5]

It was therefore scarcely surprising that the Secretary of State rejected the African request for a special investigator and authorized the Governor to proceed with the new scheme for the non-professional African staff.[6]

From the ACS to the Local Civil Service (LCS)

About the same time as African clerks were ventilating their grievances, Asians had also become alarmed about their

---

[1] C.O. 536/185/40035, BGAEA to S. of S., 5.29.35.

[2] Ibid., C.O. minutes on Governor to S. of S., Confidential, 6.24.35 and the attached petition.

[3] Ibid., minute by Garson, 7.4.35.

[4] Ibid., minute by Campbell, 7.9.35.

[5] Ibid., minute by Flood, 7.6.35.

[6] Ibid., S. of S. to Governor, Confidential (Draft), 7.18.35.

prospects in the UCS. The existing structure excluded them from many higher posts and privileges normally reserved for the Europeans. Thus they were increasingly in favor of a non-racial meritocracy entered through competitive examinations and with regulations equally applicable to Africans, Asians and Europeans.[1]

In 1936, the racial structure of the UCS was publicly denounced by several Africans, using the immigrants' own mouthpiece, the <u>Uganda Herald</u>, to refute misconceived and malicious notions about the Africans and to persuade the public to show a more charitable attitude towards them. S. K. Lukabi wondered why the African school-leavers were paid such pitiful salaries not exceeding shs. 20/- p.m. His own guess was that either the Government stood on extremely shaky financial grounds or else the African learners were hopelessly incompetent. He implored "the thinking public and...those in authority" to employ fewer Africans but pay them at least a living wage. Lukabi outlined to the country's would-be employers the housing, transport, food, marriage and other problems confronting the African workers.[2]

In May 1936 E. Musoke criticized the Protectorate Government for its meanness and unsympathetic attitude towards "Baganda civil servants." He cast the Government, which refused the Baganda equal pay for equal work and which "blindly but highly" esteemed the Indians, as the villain that perpetrated their sufferings. Musoke could not stomach the fact that the British favored the Asian staff at the expense of the Africans:

> I think East Africans are very much suffering from flooding of the Indian civil servants. Indians are ruled subjects and as such they must serve in their own country and let East Africa be served by Europeans and Africans or with a very few Asiatics as far as the Asiatic languages are concerned.

Finally, he argued that the root cause of dishonesty among the African employees was their pathetic salaries and this should be

---

[1] The <u>Uganda Herald</u>, 1.24.34, p. 18; ibid., 9.5.35, p. 19.

[2] Ibid., 1.15.36., p. 29, letter from S. K. Lukabi.

urgently rectified by proper remuneration for them.[1] From such letters to the press it is clear that educated Africans in Uganda felt antipathy against Asians as much as a consequence of conflicts in the UCS as of Asian domination of the retail trade.

Many African and Asian tribulations were allayed during the noteworthy governorship of Philip Mitchell (1935-1940). He immediately and sincerely addressed himself to the task of localizing the UCS. In late 1935 standing instructions were issued to severely restrict the overseas recruitment of what he called "the very expensive supervisory staff." He further directed that no vacancies were to be filled without fully exploring local alternatives. Mitchell, interestingly, was the first Governor to publicly acknowledge that housing for the African staff was a government responsibility. Moreover, during 1936 plans for introducing a Local Civil Service (LCS) were already under consideration.[2]

His plans for creating a LCS would have been futile without progress in African education. Hence, his initiative resulted in the visit of the Earl de la Warr Commission to Uganda in early 1937. African discontent, particularly over the salary scales, had not yet abated under Mitchell. The BGAEA seems to have placed its trust in Mitchell to ameliorate their conditions and therefore had apparently ceased petitioning the Government. However, the BGAEA was able to exploit most effectively the visit of the de la Warr Commission. Simon B. K. Musoke and Paulo N. Kavuma, encouraged by the unexpected friendliness of the Commissioners, poured out all the woes of the African employees and loaded the Commissioners with copies of the past petitions of the BGAEA.[3]

---

[1] Ibid., 5.20.36, p. 17, letter from E. Musoke. That this problem was not confined to Uganda may be seen from W. M. Macmillan, "The Importance of the Educated African," in Journal of African Society, vol. 33, no. CXXXI, 1934, p. 139.

[2] Legco summary, 11.2.36; ibid., 11.9.36, pp. 6-7.

[3] Interviews: Kavuma and Musoke, Kla., 1970. See also, the Uganda Herald, 7.2.41, p. 13. Musoke's role in effectively presenting African grievances to the Commissioners was revealed in

These efforts were not made in vain. Many of the most persistent African arguments reappeared in the report of the Commission in September 1937. For example, the now discredited low salaries were further excoriated in the report:

> High character is not encouraged by low pay. It is no good educating an African to a high standard and then asking him to live as he would have if he had never left his old environment. There is a disposition in some quarters to assume that an African need never be paid more than 20s. or 30s. a month.

The Commission recommended a minimum salary of 73/- per month for all white-collared African employees who hoped to get married and have children. The BGAEA's foreboding that the diluted salary scales would force many Africans to defect from the Government had begun to materialize. This was indeed annoying to those European officials who had labored to train the Africans but had to lose them because they lacked the authority to pay them better salaries. To arrest this grave and undesirable process, the Commission urged the East African Governments to coordinate their future higher education policy with "a salary scale providing an adequate living wage at the bottom and a complete ladder to the grade at present staffed by European University graduates." This would restore African confidence in the Civil Service and provide them with some incentive to make it their lifelong career. But it was specified that the Africans should not receive the same emoluments as the expatriate staff since no colonial government could possibly afford such an establishment.

However, the Africans had managed to convince the Commissioners that early marriage was of paramount importance in their society. The Africans had contended that their efficiency at work was inseparable from the stability of their home and social life, a point of view accepted by the Commission:

---

a profile on him, on the occasion of his appointment to a <u>saza</u> chieftaincy.

> It is likely to be a severe moral and psychological strain upon students if they must postpone marriage until the completion of a course of studies which carries them well over the age of twenty. Their moral well-being would therefore seem to require a salary which may enable them to marry upon a reasonable standard of living soon after they complete their studies.[1]

The Commission's report clearly established a strong case for a fresh look at the African salaries. At the Governor's behest two local committees probed deeper into the entire question of skilled and unskilled African labor, in 1937 and 1938. (Ingham, 1958) In August 1938 Mitchell announced that "improvements in a number of directions" would shortly be implemented for the African staff.[2]

The LCS - An African Victory

The policy of Africanizing the clerical service had been decisively adopted in 1929. Since then, owing to the many and varied setbacks examined earlier, the Asian influence in the clerical branch could not be erased. Seventy-two Asian clerks were recruited between 1929 and 1939, albeit on a temporary or contract basis.[3] However, it is incontrovertible that, in 1937, Philip Mitchell and the Earl de la Warr Commission, acting partly in response to the BGAEA's pressures, started the tremors that would finally upset the three-tier, racially-oriented Civil Service of Uganda.

At long last in late 1939, the relentless campaign for improvement waged by the African leadership showed at least the symbolic signs of victory. By this time, the BGAEA had renamed itself the Uganda African Civil Servants' Association (UACSA) so

---

[1] Higher Education in East Africa, H.M.S.O., Col. no. 142, 1937, pp. 27-29.

[2] Legco summary, 8.16.38, p. xiv.

[3] See Asiatic CSA, File no. 51/1, Memorandum to the Lidbury Commission, 4.15.53.

as to be at least nominally the equal of the Uganda European Civil Servants Association and the Uganda Asiatic Civil Servants Association.[1] In November 1939 Mitchell declared that "the proposals for much needed improvements in the terms of service of certain classes of our African employees" had been completed. For Mitchell this was fulfillment of a personal undertaking made to the representatives of the UACSA two years earlier. He paid tribute to its leaders who had "behaved with admirable restraint and public spirit while the inevitably protracted investigations and inquiries were being carried out."[2]

The new scheme mentioned by the Governor was a reference to the proposed L.C.S. Though the African endeavors were absolutely central in procuring this revision, it is quite likely that certain other factors came into play as well. The Asians had lately begun to describe themselves as "immigrant natives" in order to justify their continued claim to the UCS.[3] Many of them were locally born and educated in Kenya or Uganda and their ties with India were weakening. It was no longer necessary for a growing number of them to take overseas leave in India either for recuperation or reunion with their families.[4] Moreover, both Asian and African representatives had expressed their desired to have a single civil service for all the three races. Now the Government could kill two birds with one stone. On the one hand, it could trim Asian privileges and salaries thus reducing them from an expatriate to a local level. On the other hand it could

---

[1] The Uganda Herald, 3.22.39; interviews: Musoke and Kagobya, Kla., 1970.

[2] Legco summary, 11.29.39, p. 36.

[3] C.O. 685/25, Exco minutes, 9.24.38.

[4] See Report of the Commission on The Civil Services of Kenya, Tanganyika, Uganda and Zanzibar, H.M.S.O., 1948, Col. no. 223, para. 47. In Tanganyika a L.C.S. was introduced in 1942 for these reasons, although Asian recruitment on overseas terms had stopped in 1932.

elevate African conditions and pay by bridging the gulf between the African and Asian services. This arrangement would be expected to be satisfactory to the two groups and less costly to the Government. With the birth of the LCS in 1940, the UACSA could breathe a sigh of relief: an important battle had been won but the long struggle for complete equality remained to be waged until Uganda's independence (1962) and even after. (Motani, 1975)

Conclusion

The salient points that have emerged from this first detailed account of the African Civil Service need to be emphasized. First, the hitherto underestimated and neglected African civil servants find their proper place in the history of indigenous protestors, reformers and resistors of the colonial era. Educated Africans were led to believe that they would replace the Asians in the subordinate service within a short time. But when this failed to materialize, during the early 1920s, African clerks and interpreters became disillusioned. Frustration with bad conditions of service and poor prospects in general did not go unchallenged. Their feeling of frustration against the British Government gave birth to the first inter-tribal association, the British Government Native Employees Association (BGNEA), in 1923, which was renamed the Uganda African Civil Servants' Association in the 1930s. British equivocation regarding African status in the Civil Service and the preferential treatment granted to the Asian staff made the BGNEA deeply suspicious of the Protectorate Government and resentful of the Asian staff. This African pressure group remained very active throughout the interwar period and equipped many of its leaders with political and organizational experience. As the more ambitious African clerks left the Protectorate Service, they took with them this experience, and perhaps more important, a distrust of the British and an acute dislike of the Asians. While the British had regarded the short African tenure in the government offices as useful training for future chiefs, to the Africans this period had provided a political awakening.

Second, the generally accepted view that African leaders' dislike and distrust of the Asians was primarily derived from Asian-African friction in the province of trade needs to be mollified. Many of the future chiefs and politicians had early brushes with Asians in the colonial bureaucracy. For example, of the former Protectorate clerks, Paulo Kavuma and Mikaeri Kintu served as the Kabaka's <u>Katikiros</u> (chief ministers); S. W. Kulubya and Y. K. Lubogo became the first African mayors of Kampala and Jinja, respectively; many more attained lesser and greater chieftaincies; and Y. S. Bamuta, better known for his trade agitation and commercial rivalry with the Asians (Apter, 1967), had long been an anti-Asian militant clerk in the 1920s.

Finally, the Uganda Civil Service stands out as an index of the wider clashes between the interest groups in Uganda's multi-racial, colonial society. Study of these conflicts and the manner in which they were resolved increases our knowledge and understanding of racialism and colonialism.

REFERENCES

Adu, A.L., *The Civil Service in New African States*, London, 1965.
———, *The Civil Service in Commonwealth Africa*, London, 1969.

Apter, D.E., *The Political Kingdom in Uganda*, Princeton, 1967.

Cairns, H.A.C., *Prelude to Imperialism*, London, 1965.

Ehrlich, "Some Social and Economic Implications of Paternalism in Uganda," *J.A.H.*, iv, 2 (1963), pp. 275-285.

Fallers, L.A. (ed.), *The King's Men*, O.U.P., 1964.

Ghai, D.P. and Y. P. Ghai (eds.), *Portrait of a Minority*, O.U.P., Revised edition, 1970.

Heussler, Robert, *Yesterday's Rulers*, London, 1963.

Higher Education in East Africa, H.M.S.O., Col. no. 142, 1937.

Iliffe, John, *Tanganyika Under German Rule, 1905-1912*, Cambridge, 1969.
———, in I.N. Kimambo and A.J. Temu (eds.), *A History of Tanzania*, E.A.P.H., Nairobi, 1969.

Ingham, K., *The Making of Modern Uganda*, London, 1958.

Jefferies, C.J., *The Colonial Empire and its Civil Service*, Cambridge, 1938.

Lonsdale, J.M., "Some Origins of Nationalism in East Africa," *J.A.H.*, ix, 1(1968), pp. 119-146.

Low, D.A., *Buganda in Modern History*, London, 1971.
———, *The Mind of Buganda*, London, 1971.

Low, D.A. and R.C. Pratt, *Buganda and British Overrule 1900-1955*, London, 1960.

Morris, H.S., *The Indians in Uganda*, London, 1968.

Motani, Nizar A., "Makerere College: A Study in Colonial Rule and Educational Retardation in Uganda, 1922-1940," Paper presented at the African Studies Association of America Annual Meeting, Boston, 1976, and to be published in *African Affairs*, January, 1978.
———, "The Growth of an African Civil Service in Uganda, 1912-1940," London, Ph.D. thesis, 1972, Ch. 1. A detailed account of the British search for subordinate personnel.

_____, "The Ugandan Civil Service and the Asian Problem, 1894-1972," in Michael Twaddle (ed.), Expulsion of a Minority: Essays on Ugandan Asians, Athlone Press, London, 1975.

Mulira, E.M.K., Troubled Uganda, Fabian Pamphlet, 1950.

Pratt, R.C., "Administration and Politics in Uganda, 1919-1945," in Vincent Harlow and E.M. Chilver (eds.), History of East Africa, vol. II, London, 1965.

Report of the Commission on the Civil Services of Kenya, Tanganyika, Uganda, and Zanzibar, H.M.S.O., 1948.

Richards, A.I. (ed.), East African Chiefs, London, 1960.

Roberts, A.D., "The Sub-Imperialism of the Baganda," J.A.H., III 3(1962), pp. 435-450.

Symond, Richard, The British and Their Successors: A Study in the Development of the Government Services in the New States, London, 1966.

Thomas, H.B. and R. Scott, Uganda, London, 1935.

Twaddle, Michael, "The Bakungu Chiefs of Buganda under British Colonial Rule, 1900-1930," J.A.H., x, 2(1969), pp. 309-322.

_____, Politics in Bukedi, 1900-1939, London, Ph.D. thesis, 1967.

Watson, "A History of Church Missionary Society High Schools in Uganda, 1900-1924: The Education of A Protestant Elite," Ph.D. thesis (University of East Africa), 1968.

Maxwell School

Founded in 1924, the Maxwell School for fifty years has been training and educating young men and women for public service and academic careers. From the beginning the School has included all the University's social science departments, and this combination of professional and academic programs has enriched the content of all Maxwell's offerings. In addition to the traditional social science disciplines (Anthropology, Economics, Geography, History, Political Science, and Sociology), the School provides interdisciplinary degree programs in International Relations, Public Administration, the Social Sciences, and Urban and Regional Planning. Of the School's approximately 700 candidates for advanced degrees about half are in the traditional social science departments and the other half in interdisciplinary programs.

Today, the Maxwell School has 130 faculty members and approximately 700 students enrolled in graduate degree programs. Each year approximately 225 students receive master's degrees and 70 students Ph.D. degrees. In the three-year period, fall 1970 through spring 1973, Maxwell faculty members authored 78 books, 53 monographs, 296 articles, and 133 conference papers.